The Writer's Mindset

Chris Hall

The Writer's Mindset

6 Stances That Promote Authentic Revision

Foreword by **Linda Rief**
Heinemann · Portsmouth, NH

Heinemann
145 Maplewood Avenue, Suite 300
Portsmouth, NH 03801
www.heinemann.com

Offices and agents throughout the world

The author and publisher wish to thank those who have generously given permission to reprint borrowed material:

Figure 2–11: Screenshot image of Katherine Johnson NASA ID: Makers. Used with permission. NASA logo: Reprinted by permission of NASA.

Figure 3–24: Great Bay map. Reprinted by permission of Great Bay Stewards and the Barrington Public Library.

Figure 5–12: "Success Kid" photograph © and ™ Laney Griner @LaneyMG; Used under license.

Page 154: Excerpts from "The Beautiful Game" from *Booked* by Kwame Alexander. Copyright © 2016 Kwame Alexander. Reprinted by permission of HarperCollins. All rights reserved.

Library of Congress Cataloging-in-Publication Data
Name: Hall, Christopher, 1971– author.
Title: The writer's mindset : six stances that promote authentic revision / Christopher Hall.
Description: Portsmouth, NH : Heinemann, [2021] | Includes bibliographical references.
Identifiers: LCCN 2021030759 | ISBN 9780325118635 (paperback)
Subjects: LCSH: Authorship—Psychological aspects. | Authors—Psychology. | Creation
    (Literary, artistic, etc.)—Psychological aspects.
Classification: LCC PN171.P83 H35 2021 | DDC 808.0201/9—dcundefined
LC record available at https://lccn.loc.gov/2021030759

Editors: Tom Newkirk and Margaret LaRaia
Production Editor: Sean Moreau
Cover and Interior Designer: Vita Lane
Typesetter: Gina Poirier Design
Manufacturing: Val Cooper

Printed in the United States of America on acid-free paper
1 2 3 4 5 VP 25 24 23 22 21
September 2021 Printing

For Trisha, Emma, and Eliza,
who buoyed me with their optimism.

Contents

Acknowledgments

There were many times I was living this book as I was writing it—muddling through some of the same revision challenges described in the pages ahead. There were moments when I ached for optimism, when the chapter felt flat, when the ideas didn't coalesce, when I couldn't see my way through. Fortunately, the myth of the solo writer chugging away in isolation wasn't true for me; there were many people who stoked and shored up the best parts of my writer's mindset when I needed it most.

Ellin Keene, maven of action research (and reading, and student engagement, and aviation . . .) was a cheerleader for these ideas when they were first forming. As our fearless leader on the Heinemann Fellows, Ellin nudged my thinking about revision from the very beginning with her positive spirit and thoughtful questioning. Ellin's laugh is one of the warmest, most welcoming sounds you can hear.

To the 2016–2018 Fellows—Katie Charner-Laird, Tricia Ebarvia, Ian Fleischer, Kate Flowers Rossner, Kent Haines, Aeriale Johnson, Anna Osborn, Dr. Kim Parker, Hollis Scott, Tiana Silvas—I am in awe of you as teachers and writers. Our two-year think tank was the best professional development and incubator of ideas that I could have asked for.

Linda Rief, middle school language arts guru, treasured colleague, and my mentor teacher all those years ago, thank you for giving me the inspiration (and the occasional gentle prod) that practicing teachers are the voices that need to be heard in the discussions—and books—about literacy instruction.

To the members of our Oyster River Action Research crew—Cathy Baker, Sue Bissell, Corey Blais, Erin Bobo-Caron, Clay Cahoon, Cristina Dolcino, Heather Drew, Pam Felber, Michelle Fitzhenry, Candace French, Emily Geltz, Ann Gordon, Nate Grove, Trisha Hall, Barb Jasinski, Jaclyn Jensen, Sarah Larson-Dennen, Andrea Lawrence, Dave Montgomery, Kai Schidlovsky, Alison Smith, Jen Show, Maggie Trier, Michele Vizzo, Aaron Ward, Jen Weeks, Val Wolfson, and Kate Zimar—our deep dives into your research questions helped my own ideas take shape, as well. In particular, thanks to Sarah for welcoming my fifth-grade mentors into her classroom and to Emily for sharing her journey (and honest challenges) of trying genreless writing with her students. Not everyone would have let them write about farts.

To the administrators I've been fortunate to work with, Todd Allen and Jim Morse, your support of teacher research in our district has been tremendous. Jay Richard and Bill Sullivan, thank you for believing in teachers and your continual support of all the great work in our building.

My fifth-grade colleagues at Oyster River Middle School—Sunny Sadana, Sara O'Brien, and most of all, Dave Montgomery, my teaching partner for many years—worked with me on many of these writing projects. Dave's a creative whirlwind, and many of my best—and wackiest—teaching ideas were hatched alongside him. They usually involved wearing wigs.

Now that I've moved to eighth-grade language arts, I'm privileged to work with an amazing team of teachers: Val Wolfson, Jay Derick, Lisa Miller, Julia Widelski, and Kim Donovan. The shift to upper middle school has been a huge one, and collaborating with Kim and Val on a variety of language arts and social studies projects has been the highlight of the move. Thanks to Jay, Laura Fant, and Dave Ervin for the great pictures from the Evening of Writing and Music (and to Dave for the collaborations over the years that inspired so much wonderful student writing).

Mike Anderson, our runs through the woods around Durham have always sparked my thinking about writing, revision, and teaching. Your feedback on teacher language and the anecdotes about risk-taking were especially helpful. Thanks for always making yourself available to hash out ideas—whether it was across the yard, on the deck, or hoofing it up some hill. Bena Kallick, thank you for sharing your thoughts on the overarching ideas of the book and its connections to Habits of Mind.

Maggie Fitzhenry, for her dynamite illustrations of students in the "thought bubbles" in Chapters 2 through 7. It was a pleasure having Maggie as a student in fifth and eighth grades—and now an honor to have her artwork grace these pages.

Michael Penney, for coming up with some wonderful photos, despite the difficult subject (yours truly).

Louise Buckley from the University of New Hampshire, for hunting down some last-minute resources. You want something found, you call a reference librarian like Louise!

Thanks to the Heinemann crew: Catrina Swasey—for handling my countless emails and rookie mistakes with grace and patience. Roderick Spelman—for reaching out, putting my mind at ease, and placing me in the best of hands with Tom. Vita Lane, Suzanne Heiser, and Gina Poirier for a knockout cover and interior design. Beth Tripp and Cindy Black for their amazing eyes for detail (and dangling modifiers). Thanks to you both for making my words so much better. Sean Moreau and Patty Adams—for guiding the book through the final stages of production. Elizabeth Silvis—for her ideas (and enthusiasm) about getting this book into educators' hands. Vicki Boyd—for your leadership, humble wisdom, genuine listening, and taking a chance on *two* Durham teachers in that cohort of Fellows.

Thanks to Tom Newkirk, for coaching me through the final innings and reminding me that "perfect is the enemy of good." Our chats about writing as we hiked in the White Mountains (or just walked the neighborhood) are the best professional development I can think of. The Wreck a Draft activity came from a suggestion of Tom's as we climbed Mount Chocorua. I should probably keep a running audio record of these hikes, to capture all the rich ideas that spill out of Tom.

A special thanks to Margaret LaRaia, for believing in these ideas and helping to sculpt them with such insightful comments and gently probing questions. You kicked this whole project into motion during that one cold-brew–fueled afternoon when you surprised me with "I think you might have a book here." You were a true thought partner, Margaret, as you helped me stay flexible and navigate big shifts in the structure of the book. Each belief and practice—and everything in between—was nudged in the right direction because of you.

To my former students at Georgetown Middle School, Taipei American School, and Oyster River Middle School, thanks for giving me a window into your minds as writers. It continues to be a joy and an honor to work with you as you share your writing lives with me through your drafts.

To my Uncle Chuck, for being the first writer I knew (and for still going strong). To my Aunt Pat, my in-laws (Bill Sutphen, Mary Lou Sutphen, Susie Gutpelet, and Herb Gutpelet), and my mom and dad for rooting me on, as you always have.

To Matt Collins, for celebrating this project and inquiring about it during our many backpacking trips and snowshoeing excursions. You spurred my thinking with your tales of revision in the world of earth science, and your support (and title suggestions) kept me going.

To Emma and Eliza, for your words of encouragement. I look forward to seeing your writing continue to blossom.

Most of all, to Trisha, who was a sounding board for many of these ideas and offered an elementary educator's perspective (not to mention opening up her third-grade classroom to my middle school revision mentors). She is the finest teacher I know.

Foreword: Room 201

Linda Rief

In the Fall of 2019, a few months into the school year, I stopped in at the middle school, wandering down the hall to see my former colleagues and Chris Hall, now the eighth-grade teacher in Room 201. When I stepped through the door, *my* door, all eyes turned to me. Twenty-plus eighth graders stared at me. Who is this person? What is *she* doing here? I stared back at them: Who are *you*? What are *you* doing here? This is *my* room. It was one of my rooms for more than forty years in this building. Heads bent back into their writing. Room 201. This was *their* room, with *their* teacher, Mr. Hall.

Chris Hall. I couldn't have been happier that he was taking over for me. He is a positive, compassionate, intelligent, energetic educator who brings both idealism and realism to all that he does. He is a person of the highest integrity, who still makes me proud to be a fellow teacher.

Almost twenty-five years ago Chris interned with me. He was my partner from the moment he stepped into the classroom. He worked tirelessly to plan, share, and reshape ideas with me. He integrated new content and techniques into numerous existing curricula designs. His awareness of the diversity needed in content, in strategies, in techniques, and in learning styles for adolescents was, and still is, so impressive. He brought a vibrancy to the classroom that I see carried into this book.

Chris views the world as his classroom, always noticing things that intrigue him and that might capture the attention of his students. I recall one example during his internship that vividly illustrates his thinking and actions as a teacher and as a human being.

We were studying the Holocaust through the lens of children and what happens when they have few to no choices in their lives. "I know so little about this," Chris said. "I need to know more." He researched a weeklong fellowship at the Holocaust Museum in Washington, D.C., applied, was accepted, and learned all he could about this horrific time period.

A few months later, when he returned from winter break after visiting Philadelphia, he couldn't wait to tell me about a chance meeting with Isaiah

Zagar, an artist who had covered a block of buildings in ceramic tile and looping ribbons of mirror—whole buildings, five stories high, were now mosaic art pieces. For a day, Chris apprenticed himself to Isaiah to learn what he was doing.

For Chris, always the learner, always wanting to know more, he connected these two experiences and couldn't wait to share with his students.

"What if we figure out how to build a mosaic in conjunction with studies of the Holocaust?" Chris suggested. His excitement was energizing and contagious. We spent the entire last quarter of that year working on writing, reading, listening to guest speakers who had survived the horrors of a death camp, and constructing a four-by-eight–foot mosaic that represented what students had learned about the Holocaust and other human rights issues. The experience was challenging yet invigorating. All the kids were engaged and changed by what they had learned. It would not have happened without Chris.

By reading Chris' book, you are apprenticing yourself to him. He will become your colleague, your partner, as he so thoughtfully and so unpretentiously describes what you might try with your students to help them see how to make their writing better.

In our middle school department meetings, we often looked to Chris for guidance as a collaborator as we developed and reframed curricula. I constantly nudged Chris to write a book. "Other teachers need to hear how you've enhanced and reshaped ideas from all you've learned and tried in your classroom . . . I need your book." And now he has done it: *The Writer's Mindset: Six Stances That Promote Authentic Revision.*

Essentially, the book focuses on revision—the heart of what makes writing powerful and compelling. But this book is about so much more. It is about helping our students develop the mindsets essential to writers who learn and grow *with* each other and *from* each other. The mindsets that Chris describes here, so eloquently and clearly, drive students deeper into their thinking and writing. He teaches them, and us, how to think like writers by noticing and paying attention to what they do during the process of crafting a piece of writing. Metacognition—how do you know what you know? As Chris articulates in this book, "Students embracing metacognition become aware of their own reactions to their drafts and their own writing moves." When students develop this mindset, they are internalizing the kinds of things they might try, or might avoid, in another piece of writing. They are moving their writing forward.

Rethinking one's writing also comes from reading like a writer—noticing that the writer did something that influenced you, the reader—making you wonder and ask, *how'd she do that? I'd like to try that in my own writing.* A mindset that further helps students develop as writers.

Chris demonstrates how seemingly small, but hugely meaningful, shifts in our beliefs and practices make a difference in the writing lives of our students. Accessible and sensible ideas that move kids as writers from "I like it the way it is" to "I tried using the first person *I* to make it more personal, and I changed all the verbs to the present tense. I feel like it says what I want it to say so much better. . . . I'm really proud of all I did to make this my best writing yet."

Roald Dahl once said, "By the time I am nearing the end of a story, the first part will have been reread and altered and corrected at least one hundred and fifty times. I am suspicious of both facility and speed. Good writing is essentially rewriting. I am positive of this" (Heard 2002).

"Suspicious of both facility and speed." Chris agrees. Revision that promotes growth is not about speed or compliance or coercion. Authentic revision takes time and comes from developing a personal desire, an enthusiasm to make what one wants to say the best it can be. Revision comes from recognizing and understanding, for oneself, why a piece of writing is meaningful and significant to the writer. And like an athlete or musician, we get better with practice, learning the moves and techniques with more facility by writing again and again.

Chris seamlessly weaves in two essential ideas that remain central to my thinking as an educator: we must write with our students, and we must model our thinking aloud as we write.

It is worth repeating: we must write with our students, and we must model our thinking aloud as we write. When our students see us as writers, they trust us when we point out what they did well. They consider our questions to them as legitimate curiosity. They take our suggestions seriously. This is central to Chris' book—developing a mindset for authentic revision for ourselves, as well as our students.

As I read Chris' thinking, it strikes me again and again—we must make the time to talk with each other about our beliefs, our ideas, our practices, and our wonderings. These discussions are the most important conversations we have. Yet, if that doesn't happen as often as we would like, we must ask those questions of ourselves and of our students.

Chris made time for these conversations by doing action research and working with colleagues as a Heinemann Fellow in 2017. He looked closely at one aspect of teaching writing that really concerned him—revision. He asked himself if his teaching practices sparked a culture of revision, or if he was "unintentionally feeding revision resistance." Reading Chris' words makes me realize there is so much I could have done differently in Room 201 to move students forward in their writing. We cannot, we must not, become complacent and satisfied that what we are doing, and how we are doing it, is the best we have to offer our students. Even those of us who write books for other teachers must admit that as a book goes to print, we have already begun to rethink and revise our teaching mindsets.

This is exactly who Chris is: the reflective practitioner who acts on what he learns from his students, from other professionals, from his experiences with adolescent writers, and as a writer himself.

I stepped out of the classroom in June of 2019. Forty years as a learner, most of it with eighth graders. I miss their energy and their complacency, their curiosity and their boredom, their maturity and their childishness, their confidence and their insecurities.

On that last week of school, I was still trying to *get through* to my student, Leah, who gave *some* reading and writing her best effort, and other times, shrugged off everything. "I'm still worried about you," I said. "What could I have done differently to make it better for you?" She gave me her best eighth-grade stance: hand on the hip, head bent into a rhetorical question mark, eyes shifting in resigned boredom from me to the ceiling, from the ceiling to me, from me to the ceiling. With the collective sigh of hundreds of eighth graders, she said: "It's hard working with teenagers, isn't it?"

You bet it is, I thought, and I loved every minute of it.

Chris Hall stepped into Room 201 in August of 2019 wanting to learn from eighth graders. I wish I was still there, trying so many of the things I learned from him as I read this book. *You* are still in the classroom. How lucky you and your students are as you learn how to develop the stances central to a mindset for growing your writing and the writing of your students with Chris as your guide. You will understand what Naomi Shihab Nye means when she says: "Now I see *revision* as a beautiful word of hope. It's a new vision of something. It means you don't have to be perfect the first time. What a relief!" (Heard 2002).

Reimagining Revision

From a Stage to a Mindset

"*I like it the way it is.*" As a writing teacher, I groan when I hear my students say this. It's the verbal equivalent of that giant, capitalized declaration etched into many of their writing pieces: THE END (see Figure 1–1). Whether uttered or written, whether delivered with a defiant scowl or offered hesitantly, the message is the same: *This piece is not changing. This work site is closed, and no renovations will be made. No "revision"—no "reseeing" of this writing—is happening, period.*

> my dad. We ended up throwing it into the woods and alls well (when she brought it back we determend it was a wood chuck.) that ends well.
>
> The End

Figure 1–1 Student Story with the Classic Ending

What's Behind Students' Resistance to Revision?

Maybe it should be no surprise, this resistance. If we're honest, it shouldn't be a shock to hear our students balking at revision. Revision is tough for *all* writers, for lots of valid reasons.

A Big Ask

Let's face it: revision takes significant effort and time. For most of us, it can be a daunting task just to *complete a draft*, let alone revise it. Once we finish a draft, it can feel agonizing to have to let go of parts or change them, when we know how much work it takes (as the surveys from Cayden and Eli attest). (See Figures 1–2 and 1–3.)

Take, for instance, a moment with Henry, one of my fifth graders. It was around November during writing workshop, and we were conferring on his memoir about getting a new puppy. Henry had lots of difficulty getting his

Figure 1–2   Cayden's Thoughts on Revision

How do you feel about revising? Do you like to revise your writing? Why or why not?

I don't like revising because it takes to much time because it is a vary frushrating time and it's hard

Figure 1–3   Eli's Thoughts on Revision

How do you feel about revising? Do you like to revise your writing? Why or why not?

I don't really care I mean like it takes up time sweet time wich is my eppinion.

ideas on the page early in the year—on his September self-reflection, he admitted, "i haet writeing"—but since then he had come so far. He was initiating pieces more on his own, quickwriting along with our class, and now he was eager to show me how he had written nearly a full page about his first moments with Pippin, his new pet. He lit up as he described Pippin's wild play leaps, his painfully sharp puppy teeth, and how his family fell in love when they first laid eyes on him at the shelter. This enthusiasm was a huge achievement—even if many of his ideas hadn't made it on the paper yet. "What did Pippin look like as a puppy?" I asked after a bit, broaching any revisions gently, carefully. After Henry's animated description of his "fluffy fur ball," I added, "I wonder if you might include some of what you just said so that readers might 'see' it, too." Like a cloud passing in front of the sun, the gleam in Henry's eyes dulled at the first whiff of feedback. I could almost see his heels start to dig in. *I like it the way it is.*

I wanted to have an exchange of ideas—a give-and-take so that Henry could see the options and power he had as a writer—but he was already feeling defeated. For Henry, I had suddenly morphed into just another adult telling him, yet again, to make changes, when just finishing a draft was a formidable task in itself.

No Simple Path

There are no easy solutions, guarantees, or formulas for revision. Often, we can sense a piece of writing needs to be improved, but we're unclear about what do to next. (See Figures 1–4 and 1–5.)

Ian, Kalen, and so many of our other student writers don't feel like they have any strategies for revision, or they can't see a path forward. They might have a vague—or painfully acute—sense that their draft is lacking, but they're at a loss about how to proceed.

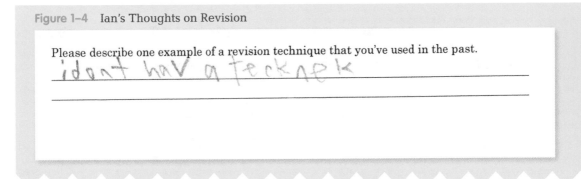

Figure 1–4   Ian's Thoughts on Revision

Please describe one example of a revision technique that you've used in the past.

idont haV a tecknek

Figure 1–5   Kalen's Thoughts on Revision

How do you feel about revising? Do you like to revise your writing? Why or why not?

Its okay, I just some times get frustated when I cant figure things out.

The Feedback Threat

It can feel threatening or frustrating when we get suggestions about our writing. It can feel like we've failed, that we've done it wrong, when someone asks us to make a change. (See Figure 1–6.)

Revision is a big ask even for some of my students who come to workshop loving writing and brimming with confidence. It can feel threatening or frustrating when we get suggestions about our writing. Take Lea, another fifth grader, who would practically skip to language arts class, excited to churn out another ten-page fantasy story. "My best writing is when I combine something that has already been written or created," she told me proudly in the fall. "Like the story I'm writing that's a combination of My Little Pony and The Hunger Games." Quite a wild blend, but Lea—with her rich descriptions of settings and characters—could make it work.

That is, until it came to revision. Lea was deep in an author share, reading her piece with relish, when—amid plenty of praise for her draft—some of her classmates voiced slight confusion about an aspect of the story. Lea bristled defensively. "I think it makes sense," she shot back, seeming to see the mildest of suggestions as an affront. "I think it's good the way it is."

Figure 1–6   Kate's Perceptions of Revision

How do you feel about revising? Do you like to revise your writing? Why or why not?

I don't like revising my writing because it feels like I did it all wrong. I also think revising and editing is plain boring.

I understand Lea's reaction. When we face a reader's question, our first response as writers is often exasperation. "How could you *not* get it?!" we think. Sometimes our readers don't see something in our draft that seems clear to us, or they don't react in the way we hope. This can be discouraging or downright aggravating.

Risk Aversion

Revising our writing often requires taking a risk, which is far from easy. We can feel vulnerable and unsure. We often have to cut out or alter parts we've become attached to. It's much easier to stick with comfortable, done, and "good enough." (See Figure 1–7.)

Figure 1–7   Dylan's Opinion of Revision

How do you feel about revising? Do you like to revise your writing? Why or why not?

I don't really like it because I like to hold on to alot of things like writing.

A Feeling of Compliance

Revision can feel like an act of submission as opposed to one of creativity. When we get lots of suggestions or are asked to make certain changes, it can feel like we're losing ownership of our piece. Despite our best efforts as teachers to take a gentle approach with our feedback, students can leave conferences feeling like we don't like their writing or that we're taking over control of it.

For many students like Mairtin and Jack, revision can feel like an act of compliance and capitulation rather than desire. (See Figures 1–8 and 1–9.)

Mining Tensions in My Teaching

Fortunately, there are lots of times when my students seem to almost magically take on the work of revision with gusto. I'll look up in my classroom, perhaps a month into the school year, and feel a hum of energy in our writing workshop—students are seeking one another out for ideas, excited and

Figure 1–8   Mairtin's Thoughts on Revision

How do you feel about revising? Do you like to revise your writing? Why or why not?

NO because sometimes teachers Say Change this, that and the other and you don't want to.

Figure 1–9   Jack's Feelings on Revision

How do you feel about revising? Do you like to revise your writing? Why or why not?

It's not my favorit Becouse it feels like the Teachers Don't like Your work. My feelings on Revison Becous I had a Teacher that abused Revison and Changed our Stories from O ne to anothet.

open to trying new approaches. There's a palpable buzz as my young writers are experimenting with their drafts, and virtually everyone gets swept up in the atmosphere. (See Figure 1–10.) These golden moments in my writing workshop seem to spring up organically, unexpectedly—like desert wildflowers—making me wonder: What sparked this change? How can I keep this culture of revision going—and re-create it intentionally—even when revision resistance rears its head? How do I get my students to embrace revision (or at least be more open to it)?

These questions spurred an action research inquiry in my own classroom a few years back. I had been teaching writing for a long time—passionately, pretty successfully, I thought—but this opposition to revision nagged at me. *What was at the heart of the resistance to revision in some of my students?* Using my language arts classes as a laboratory, I researched this and other questions by mining tensions in my teaching. "Tension is both an act of stretching and a state of uneasy suspense," say Ruth Shagoury Hubbard and Brenda Miller Power (2012, 23), experts on action research. "We sometimes walk a tightrope between who we are as teachers and learners and who we want to be" (23). Through my classroom research, I took a close, honest look at all the moving parts of my writing instruction—the good, the bad, and the ugly.

I had started with the tension in the way some of my students approached revision, but I began to examine tensions in my own teaching. If I was going to do some meaningful research into revision, I needed to take an honest look at my own teaching practices, to see what I was doing well (to spark the culture of revision I was sometimes seeing) and where I needed to change (where I was unintentionally feeding the revision resistance).

Figure 1–10   Students Revise Their Work with Gusto

A Digital Divide?

With more than a little uneasiness, I noticed some habits I had fallen into over the years, such as resorting to Google Drive comments more than face-to-face conferences, all in the name of efficiency. I seemed to always run out of time to confer in class, and, as the load of student drafts piled up, I was trying to get to more pieces. And I was—digitally. *Technology was playing a new role in my conferences, but was I losing some connection to my students?*

Expecting Too Much?

There were the moments when the lack of revision left me discouraged. I would read "revised" drafts that looked virtually the same as ones I'd given students feedback on and then sigh about the (seemingly) meager improvements. But, in thinking about what it took to make changes to my own writing, I wondered, *Was I forgetting how hard it was to revise? Wasn't it enough to make just a couple of significant changes in a draft? How much revision was realistic for me as a teacher to expect?*

Whose Piece Is It?

I winced as I thought of the times when (again, for efficiency's sake) I found myself giving students comments on *everything* I could think of. I told myself that there just wasn't time to respond to their writing multiple times, so I'd better not miss a thing as I chronicled every reaction in the margins. Sometimes, it was a deluge of feedback, leaving many kids looking dazed in its wake. Worse were the diligent students who took adult and peer suggestions too far, addressing every single comment until they had either overwritten their piece or killed any desire to work on it. *When we give too much feedback, or require students to address many of our suggestions, whose piece does it become? I wanted my students' revisions to be authentic and intrinsically motivated, but how much of the time were they just about compliance?*

A Mindset, Not a Set of Steps

Taking a critical look at these tensions wasn't pretty, but the soul-searching prompted some important shifts in my teaching (some of the very ideas you're reading). For all the earnest desire to improve my own teaching practice, there was something else amiss, as well. Something about how my fellow teachers and I had been taught to approach revision. We presented revision as something to face after the first draft is over. Revision was a stage in the writing process—a step right after drafting and just before editing.

But when I looked at my students at their best—and at my own experience as a writer—I realized that revision was occurring *throughout the writing*, not just after the end. Writers were stopping periodically to review and reread their words, making adjustments big and small along the way. They were pausing occasionally to notice what was working and what parts were falling short. They were aware of the moves they were trying *as they were writing*—and *why* they were trying these. "I love how I'm using questions in the first paragraph," Riley said when I conferred with her in the middle of her book review draft. "I think it will intrigue my readers and make them do a double take. Maybe they'll want to pick up my book!"

The conventional wisdom was that revision was a step near the end of the process, but I saw it happening *throughout* drafting—in micro- and macro-changes that writers like Riley were trying before, during, and after composing each line. I had been taught to wait until after the first draft was complete to have my students revise, but that seemed too late.

There was also something that didn't sit right with the whole approach of writing process and workshop. There was certainly nothing wrong with teaching students that writing is a process (i.e., prewriting, drafting, revising, editing, publishing) and showing them the structures of the workshop model (e.g., mini-lessons, conferences, shares, and predictable writing times). The problem was where these approaches focused my gaze as an educator. The way I had been taught writing process and workshop put my emphasis firmly on the writing. The spotlight—for me and my students—was always beaming down at the page.

"And where else *should* we be focusing our attention?!" you may be wondering.

Well, as it turns out, on the students themselves.

A bit less on the writing and more on the writer.

"Teach the writer, not the writing," Lucy Calkins said over thirty years ago (1986, 236). But the workshop model as I taught it—and the way I saw other colleagues teaching it—focused everything on trying to improve the writing. Our minilessons and conferences were always about ways to help students add, reorganize, reconsider, and troubleshoot the problems of the page. We taught students the power of leads, how to add dialogue, how a reader's questions can crack open a draft—all worthy lessons, for sure. But it seemed to me that there were things to be learned at the other end of the pencil—*in my students themselves*.

Revision was about what was happening in the mindset of the writer, during the writing process, not just on the page, after it was done.

When I saw my students embracing revision, it wasn't just that they knew craft moves and had learned certain writing skills (important as those are). It was their willingness—and even enthusiasm—to revise. To identify lines that were working and build from them. To be aware of their own reactions as they were writing, not just at the end of a draft. It was their openness to a new approach or tendency to take the perspective of a potential reader. Their ability to transfer one skill they had learned to a completely new genre or draft. Their willingness to take a risk in order to stretch themselves as writers.

I felt like I was stumbling upon a new definition for revision, by gazing at the students right in front of me. In short, revision was about what was happening *in the mindset of the writer, during the writing process*, not just on the page, after it was done.

Unpacking a Writer's Mindset

Influenced by the mindset research of Carol Dweck (2006) and the Habits of Mind work of Arthur Costa and Bena Kallick (2008), I began to notice and name the behaviors my students were showing when we were in the thick of a culture of revision. I was drawn to the term *stance*—coined by Kristine Mraz and Christine Hertz in *A Mindset for Learning* (2015)—because it implied a behavior my students could adopt, not a fixed, innate quality they either had or didn't have. Like a ready stance in baseball (knees bent, glove out, eyes on ball), a writing stance indicated a conscious *choice*, a way of approaching revision that we could learn and practice until it became a part of us (Mraz and Hertz 2015, xviii). Motor memory for writers.

But which behaviors—which stances—were most important for moving us beyond revision resistance? After I distilled elements from the Habits of Mind and other work, the key parts of a writer's mindset revealed themselves. Following are the stances that emerged in my classroom and students when we were at our best, our most productive—energized and open to revision.

Metacognition

Some students were aware of the decisions they were making in their drafts—*what* they were trying (their writing moves) and *why* they were trying them (their intentions). They were willing and able to see their writing, and their reactions to it, clearly and honestly—paying attention to what felt right and what sounded off in their emerging drafts. To the places in the writing that energized them or fell flat. To the lines that would be intriguing or confusing.

I could see metacognition in my student Alja, as she was thinking out loud about her personal narrative: the mortifying time when she threw a snowball in an airport parking lot and it went awry, nearly causing her family to miss a flight. Alja was uninspired by her first lines and felt they needed changing. She was pausing middraft to weigh the words of her initial lead—the effect they would have, the order in which she should present them, how much information to dole out to readers. "'It was Christmas Eve, and I was standing outside Logan Airport in the harsh, chilly weather.' I didn't really like that lead. . . . I wanted it to be more mysterious and leave people with questions, so I tried this instead: 'On the plane ride to Florida all I could think about was what had happened and wonder how a snowball could cause so much trouble.'" (See Figure 1–11.)

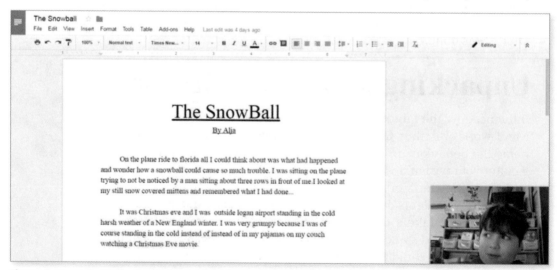

Figure 1–11   Alja Reflects Metacognitively on Her Writing

Not only did Alja create a stronger lead, but her metacognition—her self-awareness about her writing during the process—would be a resource for her to use again and again, a little voice she could listen to and learn from.

Optimism

Some students were drawn to the strengths of their draft (rather than focused on its shortcomings) and built off what was already working. This optimism helped propel them forward through the hard work of revision. In looking at the positive aspects of their writing, these students often stayed hopeful, engaged, and persistent—even when they hit difficult spots in the process.

For example, there was Elly, whose quiet optimism shone through even as she struggled to describe an oyster shell for a nature poem she was writing. She read her drafts to peers, listened to their comments, and kept trying to look at her shell with new eyes and fresh metaphors. "I was wondering how many things an oyster shell could look like. . . . I had to really think about different word choice and description. . . . I started to think that nothing was really coming 'alive,' so I had to work on revising."

Elly kept at it, adding several wonderful lines of figurative language, including one comparing the shell's layers to "a silky white staircase / Leading into an empty palace." In reflecting about the changes to her writing, she wrote, "I love to revise because it makes me feel capable to get better as I am. Also I like how even if you think your piece is perfect, it gets so much better." (See Figure 1–12.)

The optimism I saw in students like Elly wasn't some chipper, Pollyannaish attitude, but a tendency to invest their energy in what was working and to build from it. The persistence I witnessed wasn't white-knuckle tenacity—some show-grit-through-the-misery approach—but a willingness to work through the challenges of revision because the writing was worth it.

Figure 1–12 Elly Explains Why She Likes Revising

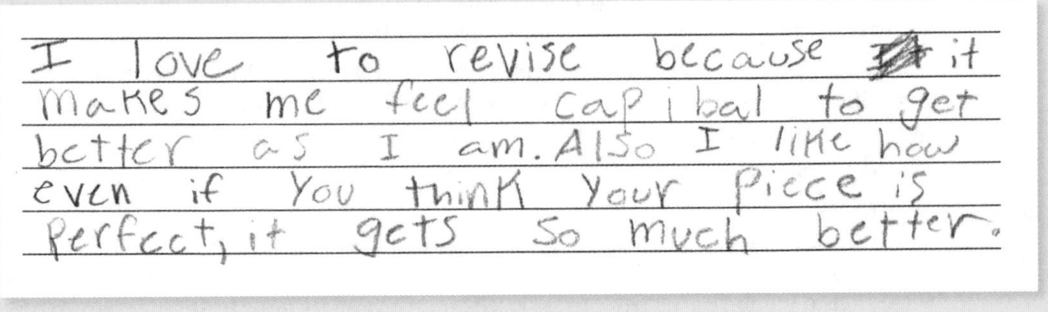

I love to revise because it makes me feel capibal to get better as I am. Also I like how even if you think your piece is perfect, it gets so much better.

Perspective-Taking and Connection with the Audience

I also noticed the students who could readily step into their readers' shoes—to see their own writing from another perspective. They anticipated what their imagined audience might need or feel while reading their draft—the places where they might be confused, the background information readers would need for clarity, the details that would be most intriguing to them. These students predicted their audience's reactions, and they listened carefully to the *actual* feedback they received from readers during conferences. These were writers thinking like readers.

I saw this perspective-taking in Riley, who told me that getting comments, suggestions, and questions from her classmates had helped her "100 percent." Riley said, "It gives me a second view (or more) on my work and can help me to make things more clear. Like in our memoirs, it may be clear to me because I was there, but to readers it may be confusing."

Perspective-taking was what made Shreya rethink what her script for a social studies presentation on Pearl Harbor needed. Her draft was written in first person—from the point of view of an American soldier facing the surprise attack—but she felt like her lines were too informational. Thinking like a reader, Shreya reflected that her script was overpacked with facts but emotionally empty. She stepped into the shoes of her soon-to-be audience, spurring some important changes to her script. "I added more feelings and voice for my character," she said, "so that the people who see [my presentation] will get facts, but also enjoy hearing how the person feels."

Flexible Thinking

I noticed students who would hold off on saying, "I'm done," who remained open to new ideas, approaches, and feedback. They showed a curiosity and confidence to try something novel with their writing—and a humility to recognize these great ideas might come from others.

Perhaps none of my students showed as great a change in flexible thinking as Lea. She started the year prickly and closed off when approached with virtually any comment about her writing. For Lea, almost any feedback—even a gently posed question—was a threat. "I really *do not* like being told what to write. I really don't," she shared on her writing self-portrait in September. "I do better writing on my own. That is why I do not like this paper." (See Figure 1–13.)

Teaching Lea reminded me what a vulnerable act writing is and how it's no easy task for a writer to trust their readers. It takes time to build a relationship, and it takes feedback that's truly supportive and helps writers to find their

Figure 1–13   Lea's Initial Feelings About Revision

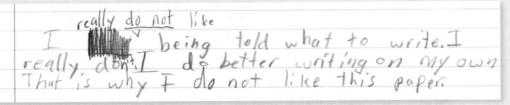

own way. Kids like Lea—all of us, really—need to know that revision doesn't mean deference or submission, but a creative back-and-forth between fellow writers. (See Figure 1–14).

As the year progressed, Lea came to see revision as challenging but well worth the effort. Taking a more open stance and listening to other ideas was a gradual—and far from easy—process for Lea, but she came to see the value in it. "Revising to me is kind of long and hard and that's why I didn't do it much," she wrote on an end-of-year survey. "But now seeing my revised memoir, I think it is important. A couple extra scratches with that graphite is okay if it will make my story better, right?"

Transfer

There were students who were conscious of the wonderful writing skills and craft moves they had previously learned and were intentionally transferring these to new pieces and situations. For instance, Jack learned about adding interior monologue—a character's inner thoughts—from one of his peers. Jack had read a piece by Alyssa, which included some conflicted and quite funny

Figure 1–14   Lea's New Attitude Toward Revision

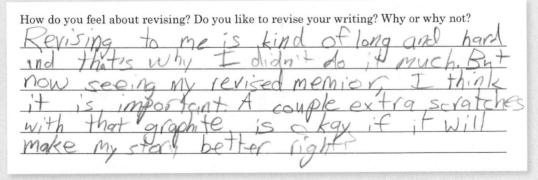

thoughts about agreeing to ride a terrifying roller coaster with her dad. After reading her story, Jack pinpointed what she had done (even if he struggled to name the craft move): "Alyssa is really good at doing the 'two voices thing' in her head—like one voice is saying, 'You're going to die!' and the other one is like, 'You can do it!'"

Jack then set out to use a similar approach in his piece about a scooter crash, a time when he misjudged a ramp at a skate park. To capture the moment when he had to decide whether to attempt a dangerous landing or leap off his scooter, Jack transferred his know-how about interior monologue: "I flew up, still on my scooter . . . the ramp was getting closer and closer . . . 'Do I stay on and maybe bash my legs? Do I jump off?' I preferred not being paralyzed, so I bailed."

Risk-Taking

Other writers play with fresh ideas and willingly take a risk to stretch beyond what they can already do. They allow themselves to be vulnerable, pushing the boundaries of what they've tried before—experimenting with new genres, narrators, story structures, endings, and more. Rather than rushing to complete a draft, they're willing to live with uncertainty in order to play with possibility.

There was Vincent, who tried writing from a point of view other than his own for the first time. In his poem "Poison Ivy," he imagined the three-leafed scourge's perspective: "I'm innocent / Don't I look friendly? / I really love playing / . . . Maybe three might be your lucky number!"

For other students, the biggest risk isn't what they will add or change, but what they will remove. For Sarah, stretching herself meant trimming down her book review. "I had to cut out the parts that gave away too much information. . . . At first I had three pages and it was so hard to cut [anything] out. It was all so important!" Removing some of her writing to make it a more manageable length was a risk for Sarah, and she was proud of how her streamlined review seemed to hook other middle school students when it was posted in our library.

I noticed my students embodying risk-taking when they presented their writing to an authentic audience—whether speaking about climate change at a community forum or acting as tour guides on Boston's Freedom Trail. (See Figures 1–15 and 1–16.)

Metacognition. Optimism and persistence. Perspective-taking and connection with our audience. Flexible thinking. Transfer. Risk-taking. Do any one of my students—do *any* writers—display all of these stances, all of the time? Of course not, but these have become powerful guideposts for us to aspire to throughout the year. Teaching the stances cultivates positive behaviors not just in writing but in any pursuit.

Figure 1–15 Students Present at a Climate Change Forum

Figure 1–16 Students Act as Tour Guides

Process Present—a New Lens on Workshop

I had taught craft lessons and writing process for years, but how could I teach *stances*, and how would these fit into writing workshop? I worried I wouldn't be able to squeeze more into my already-packed curricula and instruction, but, as it turned out, I didn't need to. Teaching the stances of a writer's mindset didn't require much more time, just a reframing of what I was already doing. I could keep my writing workshop structures; I just needed my students to think differently about revision—and about themselves.

One of the first steps was putting these stances on our collective radar. For years I had been asking students to reflect on their writing after completing a final draft—what I and my colleagues called a process history. I asked what they were proud of, what they struggled with, what changes they made in their piece. Some students groaned; others dutifully went through the motions, replying to each question. I wanted to get a window into their process as writers, but they didn't seem to find much value in it. The problem wasn't the questions, and it wasn't the students. In large part, it was the timing.

Postpiece is too late; a process history is a postmortem. For most students, rigor mortis has started to set in on their words and they are ready to move on; when a draft is finished, the piece is (cue Godfather voice) "dead to them."

Instead, I realized what my students needed was a *process present*—an awareness of their writing moves and their own stances *as they were drafting*. They needed quick metacognitive bursts during the writing process, not lengthy reflections after it was over. A process present, not a process history.

In *Mindset*, Carol Dweck points out that just introducing the notion of mindsets can be transformative. "Just by knowing about [fixed and growth] mindsets you can start thinking and reacting in new ways" (2006, 46). Mraz and Hertz liken it to putting on a "special pair of glasses," a filter through which we suddenly see our world differently (2015, 28).

Becoming aware of their own writing mindsets, my students began to see optimism in the way they identified a promising line or bounced back from a dismal quickwrite. They noticed their own metacognition in the inner voice they heard while nestled on carpet squares on the floor, pondering their next move. They paid attention to their flexibility when they paused after a minilesson, considering a new title or possibly even a whole new piece. They noticed they were anticipating their classmates' reactions to their drafts even before they dashed off to find conferring partners. They thought about their own risk-taking as they clicked away on their laptops, as they held off on saying, "I'm finished. *What should I do now?*"

The stances were suddenly everywhere—for them and for me. (See Figure 1–17.)

This book is about applying a new lens on our writing workshop practices. The goal is to see our instruction with fresh eyes: to recognize and incorporate the stances of a writer's mindset—metacognition, optimism, perspective-taking, flexible thinking, transfer, risk-taking—within our existing workshop structures.

Each of the chapters ahead begins with defining one of the stances. I then identify several core beliefs related to the stance—beliefs about its importance to writing and revision and suggestions on how to foster it in our students. Following each belief are practices—specific examples of how you can weave the stance into the minilessons and prewriting, drafting, conferring, and sharing activities you already do.

Along the way, we'll explore some subtle but seismic shifts in our teaching—ones that can spark a writer's mindset, keep students in a process present, and help them move beyond revision resistance.

Figure 1–17   Students Share and Revise with Enthusiasm

2

Metacognition

Writers Develop Through Self-Awareness

When the mind is thinking,
it is talking to itself.

—Plato

If we placed a microphone or stethoscope up to temple of a writer, what thoughts might we hear?

"When you put all the metaphor stuff out, you put the pineapple right in front of me. Once I saw it, I was like, 'That's perfect!'" Kate said, gasping with delight. She was reflecting on her draft-in-process through a "thoughtcast," a screencast about her recent metaphor poem. As part of exploring figurative language, our class had read selections from Valerie Worth's *All the Small Poems* (1987), and I had placed a variety of objects around the room, asking students to try some fresh comparisons of their own.

Kate had been drawn to the pineapple and immediately started a quickwrite. In her thoughtcast, she was reflecting on the lines she was most excited about.

"I came up with a ton of ideas the second you put [the pineapple] down. I was so happy to write about it and I really liked the lines I wrote, especially 'Spikes protect the gold inside.' . . . When I saw the spikes on it, it reminded me of a mountain, where it would be protecting gold, like where a dragon might live, protecting gold and jewels inside. . . . That line spoke to me [when I wrote it]." (See Figure 2–1.)

Kate was screencasting to me, her teacher, but she was really speaking to herself—taking note of her response to her own lines, the metaphors that resonated and struck her.

With any act of writing, there's a hidden undercurrent. We might be immersed in the physical act of writing, but below the surface, there's also our thinking about the writing and our reactions to it—our metacognition. Sometimes we're plunging headlong into writing and outracing our thinking (as in a quickwrite). Sometimes we're pausing to deliberate over our choice of words or our next move. Sometimes, like Kate, we're thinking back on the ideas we've just scrawled on the page. One thing's for sure though: we don't just wait until "The End" to consider how our piece is going. We are continually making changes on the fly and revising from the very moment we begin writing.

One of the biggest ways to help our students is by making them more aware of their thoughts about their writing as they're drafting—their head and heart reactions, what they're trying and hope to try (their decisions), and why they're doing these (their intentions). (See Figure 2–2.)

Figure 2–1   Kate's Thoughtcast

Figure 2–2   Metacognition

Belief: Teachers Need to Model Metacognition

When we're exploring the terrain of a piece of writing metacognitively, all sorts of questions and wonderings stream through our minds:

- I have the seeds of an idea—what's going well with it so far? What lines are energizing to me?

- This section doesn't feel right to me. . . . I wonder why?

- Would this part be clear to someone else?

- What's this piece really about?

This running internal dialogue is critical to good writing but often invisible to our students. Each paragraph they write includes dozens of options and decisions, but they aren't always cognizant of them. When we ask them, "What do you think is working well with your piece?" we often get an arched eyebrow or a shrug.

Other times, one of our writers is struggling with a draft because they haven't paused to consider their choices. They include a half page of description of a fast-food rest-stop meal during an otherwise exciting vacation memoir, and we ask why. "Because that's what happened!" they say. Students like these may be trying to comply with that often-heard teacher advice "Tell me more" but aren't aware of the options they have. Writers aren't stenographers, obligated to record each moment of our lives with fidelity. We need to show our students the decision-making power— the omnipotence—we writers have.

How do we do this? By helping them to be more aware of *what* they're doing (*their decisions* as writers) and *why* they're doing it (*their intentions*). To do this, we need to make the unseen revision moves visible for students, to take the silent internal commentary of writers and make it audible.

Practice: Using Minilessons to Show a Writer's Thoughts

As teachers, we can model metacognition by sharing our inner dialogue about a draft of our own.

For example, I modeled metacognition with my students by sharing a memoir I was writing about a terrible sledding accident my youngest daughter had had when she was young. (See Figure 2–4.) My think-aloud included the following:

- *Where my idea came from and why it was important to me:* "When we were all writing SOS stories last month, I was brainstorming accidents and injuries in my life. I thought of one that happened to my daughter when she was five and she got really hurt. . . . As I wrote, I realized how much emotion it brought up in me as a dad—my worry about Eliza and my feelings of guilt that I wasn't watching over her at the time."

Model Metacognition

Use a think-aloud to show the ways writers respond and talk to themselves as they are making choices throughout the process, such as

- where your idea came from and why it was important to write about;

- parts you are excited about;

- moves you are trying as a writer and why;

- aspects of the piece that still need work or that you feel unsure about; and

- what you might try next.

Figure 2–3   Model Metacognition

Figure 2–4   My Thoughtcast

- *Parts I was excited about:* "What do I think is strong so far in my piece? I like my lead, because I think I described the setting a bit, but it also has an ominous feel to it, like there's a clue about what's to come."

> The hill we usually sledded on at the Sullivans' house was behind their barn—a gentle, wide slope that stretched from their hilltop garden to their lower field. We had taken sleds and tubes down it dozens of times, squealing with laughter as we safely flew over the powder to the white stretch of field below.
>
> But that wasn't the hill the kids chose that day. On New Year's Day, for some reason, they thought they'd try the short, sudden drop-off just behind the house. Its steep sides would mean a brief but fast ride, but this hill pitched unevenly to one side. The side where the woods began.

- *Moves I was trying as a writer and why:* "I didn't have any dialogue in my first draft, because I honestly couldn't remember what anyone said; maybe it was a blur from the shock or something. I know I want to slow down the exciting parts and that having the kids talk is important, so I'm inventing some of the dialogue. I'm trying to make it realistic, to capture what each person probably sounded like and how everyone reacted."

> "What happened?!" I shouted, staring at Eliza's panicked, tear-streaked face. I looked at her bloody jacket and my mind raced.
>
> "My mouff," she said with a muffled, sobbing voice.
>
> "She just, just flew into the woods head first," stuttered Emma, steadying Eliza and walking

next to her. "We couldn't stop her." Emma looked pale, shock on her face.

"You have to let us see," said my wife Trisha, who I suddenly realized was next to me. She was kneeling in the snow in front of the girls, trying to keep her voice steady and calm.

"Nooo!" Eliza squealed, clutching her face harder. "It hurts, Momma!"

She looked at us pleading, begging us not to pry her mitten off. As if the mitten was holding everything in place.

"I'm trying to show what each person was feeling—Eliza's pain and fear, my wife trying to stay calm, my other daughter feeling bad, me kind of freaking out."

- *Aspects of the piece that still needed work or that I felt unsure about:* "I'm still uncertain about my ending—endings are hard! I know I can't just end it in the emergency room, saying she got stitches but was OK. I need to wrap up the story, but I'm not sure how. . . ."

- *What I might try next:* "One idea I have for my ending is a flash-forward: showing Eliza heading outside to sled with friends now, almost six years later. I could show the mixed emotions this brings up in me as a father—wanting to keep her safe and not let her go, but also knowing she's older and needs freedom and independence. It might also give the story a 'circular' feel, coming back around to sledding. I'll give it a try and see what all of you think."

Assuming you write alongside your students—and hopefully you do—what piece might you self-talk for them? Here are a few important considerations when choosing a piece:

- It helps if the class is already familiar with the piece and has heard it before (so your students are less concerned with understanding the content and more focused on your reflections as a writer).

- Your piece should be in progress, not a polished draft (to show your metacognition during the writing process, not after the end).

- You should share the range of your reactions—your enthusiasm for a favorite section *and* your feelings about places where you're stuck, have a question, or are frustrated.

By pulling back the curtain on our minds as writers—by modeling our decisions and intentions, midpiece—we are helping students listen for their own inner voice and reactions as they draft.

Belief: Students Need to Discover Their Writing Moves to Own Them

"What do you think is working well in your piece so far?" It's a few weeks into the school year, and I've sidled up to John, one of my fifth graders, for a conference. In front of him are a couple of pages of furious drafting about a recent (and hilarious) misadventure with the natural world: the time he accidentally ate a spoonful of ants that had invaded his cereal. John has a great start by the looks of things, but he stops and tilts his head at my question, like he hasn't considered it before. He struggles to name a single strength in his draft, even though I can see several: nice foreshadowing (the strangely open box of Cheerios; his absent-minded eating while reading a comic book), moments of rising tension ("Then I tasted something. Not like the normal honey and oat flavor. It was more . . . alive."), and a promising lead ("This just happened this past summer and the taste is still in my mouth.").

John's not alone; when we confer with our student writers and ask them to reflect on their drafts—even on the strengths in their writing—we frequently get blank stares. Students can often identify craft moves in mentor texts, but they have a harder time seeing these in their *own* writing. Often their drafts are glimmering with these wonderful moves or at least hints of them—authentic dialogue, lines of foreshadowing, funny hyperbole—but the students themselves seem unaware.

For years, I made it my mission to notice and name these "hidden gems" in my students' writing. I was inspired by Katherine Bomer, as she described the staying power when "we name something specific, something writers honestly do or at least try to do, that we can see or hear in a student's piece already" (2010, 9). This naming, she said, is "the key to teaching students something they may not have consciously realized they are doing so that they can build on it again and again" (9). I wanted to show my young writers the (sometimes hidden) potential in their words, and I made this a focus of my conferences.

Recently though, I've come to realize the transformation really occurs when *they* begin to notice and name these writing moves for themselves. We can teach students minilessons, craft strategies, and revision approaches, but a writing move isn't theirs until they see it reflected back in their writing. They can't own it until they recognize and discover it on their own.

We can help them do this by reminding our writers: *You are making decisions every step of the way in a draft.* We can help by having them pause occasionally during drafting to reflect for themselves: *What moves am I making so far? How do I think and feel about these?*

Practice: Drafting and Sharing Using Emoji Annotations

During drafting or before sharing, ask your students to read their draft to themselves, paying attention to their emotions and thoughts while moving through the text. As they reread, have them draw emojis in the margins of the text, or on sticky notes, to make note of their reactions. (See Figure 2–5.)

Emoji Annotations

Students might use emojis to show any of the following:

▸ *How they are feeling* about the topic *they're writing about:* a laughing face (😆) when reflecting on a humorous moment; a grimacing face (😬) for a painful or awkward memory

▸ *How they're feeling* about the writing *itself:* a thumbs-up (👍) for a favorite line; a confused face (😕) for a part that might need work

▸ *How they hope* the audience might feel *in different spots of the text:* an astonished face for a cliff-hanger section (😲); a thinking face (🤔) for a line they hope will leave readers intrigued

Figure 2–5   Emoji Annotations

Your students can find a rich range of emojis no matter what digital platform you use (Microsoft Word, Google Docs, etc.). Your writers may already know the shortcuts, but, if not, show them how to access different emojis so they can record a variety of reactions. For example, in Word, you can open the emoji menu, which gives students a range of emojis—over ninety—to choose from.

For a more low-tech option, just ask your students to draw their emoji reactions in the margins of a draft. Kian, a third grader, used handwritten annotating with his poem "The Thaw," about the changes he was noticing outdoors as spring arrived. (See Figure 2–6.) With each line of his draft, Kian jotted an emoji, such as smiley faces (☺) for lines that he liked—lines that captured what he was seeing in nature (e.g., "the plinking thaw has come"; "chirping birds"; "squashy mud"). He drew a neutral faces (😐) and frowns (☹) next to lines that he felt needed changing, such as "growing plants," which he thought wasn't specific enough. (As you can see, Kian even tried old-school cutting and pasting by tearing bits of sticky notes to substitute different words.)

Your students don't need to include an emoji after every line (as Kian did)—just whenever they become aware of a reaction or thought they are having as they review their writing.

No matter which approach your students use, emojis are a quick, visual way for them to reflect metacognitively on their emerging drafts.

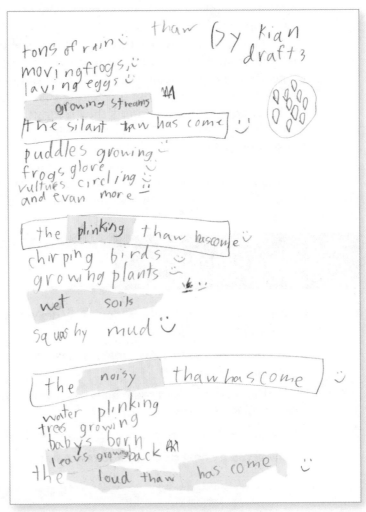

Figure 2–6   Kian's Emoji Annotations

Practice: Revising Using Revision Reflections or Thoughtcasts

One challenge with metacognition is obvious: We can't see what's happening in our students' minds as they're writing . . . *or can we?*

Rather than waiting until the end of a draft, pause students in the middle of the writing for a process present. Use a brief revision reflection to have your students share their thinking about their work so far. (See Figure 2–7.)

Questions like those in Figure 2–7 focus students on what they are attempting in the here and now—and might try in the future—instead of asking them to reevaluate the writing in their rearview mirror. A revision reflection can be as simple as a couple of questions on an exit slip or a turn-and-talk with a partner, or it could be something more involved.

One engaging way to use these questions is with a thoughtcast—a screen-cast where students reflect about their moves and decisions in real time. Using some basic screencasting tools—widely available online, many for free (such as Screencastify and Screencast-o-Matic)—have your students get meta about their writing as they're drafting. Your writers pull up their drafts on the screen (in Google Docs, Microsoft Word, etc.) and then, using the screencasting software, superimpose their audio or video commentary. (Many screencasting platforms allow students to navigate their piece while making handwritten comments and notations on key parts of their text.) See Figure 2–8 for ideas on what students can include in their thoughtcasts.

Revision Reflections

▸ **How did you come up with this idea? Why did you decide to write about it or how did it come about?**

▸ **What's going well so far? Are there parts you're excited about? (What parts, specific lines, etc.?)**

▸ **What are areas that don't seem quite right, where you're struggling to capture your ideas or emotions?**

▸ **What changes have you made so far and why did you try them?**

▸ **What will you try next as a writer to revise this piece?**

Figure 2–7   Revision Reflections

Thoughtcasts

Students can talk about the following elements in their thoughtcasts:

- ▶ **their positive reactions**
- ▶ **the moves they are making as writers—and the reasons they're trying them**
- ▶ **what they might try next**
- ▶ **why the writing piece is significant or meaningful to them**
- ▶ **how they think their readers might react**
- ▶ **when they're stuck or when something's not working**

Figure 2–8   Thoughtcasts

Thoughtcasts can include many types of reflections, including the following:

- *Students' positive reactions:* Remember Kate's thoughtcast about her pineapple metaphor poem earlier in the chapter? She honed in on the strengths of her poem and reflected on why she felt these were working well. (See her poem in Figure 2–9.) "I really liked the lines 'Lonely / Unable to show its true self' because when you look at a pineapple it looks really odd—green and brownish, with spikes all over it—and it looks *lonely*. Like you said, if you saw it in nature, would you *really* want to eat it?! It doesn't look appetizing, but once you see the inside, it looks juicy and delicious."

  Later in the thoughtcast, Kate discussed something new she had never tried before: line breaks. "I really like how I used line breaks, like how I wrote, 'Through its / Rough / Hard / Case.' I

Mission Dinner

Spewing lava

Decaying behind bright color

Frozen in time

Lonely

Unable to show its true self

Through its
        Rough
            Hard
                Case

Spikes protect the gold inside

Blades cut through the rough case

The inside shining like a thousand

Diamonds

The golden treasure

revealed....

Figure 2–9   Kate's Pineapple Poem

really wanted emphasis, and it's like these are all spat out, like there's a period after each one."

Training our eyes on what's working builds excitement and momentum, a desire to keep going. It gives writers a thread to follow, a line or idea to keep developing. By drawing their attention to the hidden gems in their draft, students begin to recognize their own competence—and perhaps build the persistence to keep going even when things get challenging. By taking note of a specific strength or craft move (such as Kate's recognition of line breaks), they can also use it, or something like it, in a future piece.

- *The moves they are making as writers—and the reasons they're trying them:* Beyond just noticing their reactions to their writing, students can start to identify *what* they are trying as writers—zooming in on a scene, playing with time, adding dialogue—and *why* they are trying it.

As he was writing a script for social studies about an important historical figure from the twentieth century, Wilson paused for metacognition. A huge soccer fan and player, Wilson was writing about Pelé. Through his thoughtcast, he became aware of the details he had added about the Brazilian superstar's career and of why these were important. According to Wilson, he was gathering more "evidence" to show how amazing Pelé truly was. "I really like the line I added—'He scored 1,281 goals out of 1,361 games.' I think that's kind of like the 'proof' 'cause I was saying Pelé was good, but I never really gave any facts or details like that." (See Figure 2–10.)

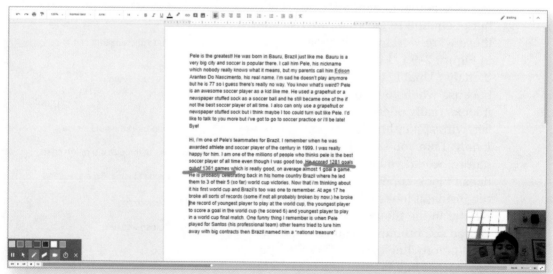

Figure 2–10 Wilson's Thoughtcast of His Piece on Pelé

Wilson also recognized that he might want to change the point of view for his script, from an objective news reporter to one of Pelé's teammates. "I'm trying to show more of people's feelings about Pelé," Wilson said, "not just a list of facts." By pausing for metacognition, Wilson realized that capturing Pelé's brilliance might involve more than just a series of statistics.

- *What they might try next:* When some writers reflect metacognitively, they are thinking about their next paragraph, like nighttime drivers considering just the stretch of road where the headlights reach. Some look back at a distinct part of their text—maybe the title or a passage of description—to consider a change. For others, metacognition helps them develop an understanding of their piece as a whole, a mental road map of their draft. They suddenly grasp the big picture—the structure of their essay, the arc of their story—and consider if they're on track.

Elsa began some biographical writing about "Women in Space" and was passionate about the topic: "I've always been into space and the background of what goes into getting people there. I've always kind of been a feminist, too, so it was a mix of both."

Midway through her process, though, she realized her focus was too narrow. "I started off just writing about [the astronaut] Sally Ride and I realized I needed to expand it to other women, too." (See Figure 2–11.)

Pausing to reflect on her draft, Elsa came to the realization that she needed to include other pioneering female figures of space exploration. As a result, her final draft ultimately included Kathryn Sullivan (the first American woman to walk in space), Margaret Hamilton (the software engineer who made the Apollo missions possible), and Katherine Johnson (the mathematician who calculated flight trajectories and was depicted in the film *Hidden Figures*).

Figure 2–11 Elsa's Presentation about "Women in Space"

Changing the structure of her piece to include a range of individuals and jobs—beyond just a single astronaut—would give a fuller picture and (in her words) a "more historically accurate" presentation of women in space.

- *Why the writing piece is significant or meaningful to them:* When we're drafting and revising, it's important to remember why we're writing or why the topic is significant to us, so we can capture the heart of the piece. It's what Nancie Atwell (1998) calls the "So what?"—the purpose, meaning, or point of the writing. As Atwell says, we often find the "So what?" in the process of writing—but only if we're reflecting back on it periodically (40).

  When Sarah was experimenting with poetry and had the freedom to choose her topic, she thought immediately of her family's fishing boat and their favorite times taking it out on Great Bay in New Hampshire. "As soon as you said to think of a place you love, I thought of our boat and all the memories I have there," she said. "It always makes me happy, and it makes me think of summer." As Sarah revised, she added vivid details about the sights, smells, and sounds aboard her boat—the "waves crashing, fish splashing . . . reel ticking, line pulling"—and she kept coming back to what the poem was about overall to her, its significance. "The thing I'm kind of struggling with," she said in her thoughtcast, "is trying to show how special our boat is to me. I'm not sure how clear it is in the poem yet and I'm trying to make it clear."

  When a student like Sarah reflects on their "So what?" they have a North Star, a reference point, to steer toward. They are less likely stray from the heart of the piece or to stick with a draft that has no real significance to them.

- *How they think their readers might react:* We write for ourselves, but it's important for us to think of how our words will be received by our audience as well. When Molly wrote a scene for her memoir "Demon Rooster," she was definitely considering—and relishing—how an added paragraph would pull in readers: "I tried making a movie in the readers' minds when I wrote: 'Suddenly I heard a rustling. I felt a chill down my back. I looked up. It was . . . so bright it was almost blinding with the moonlight on its feathers. It was about a foot and a half from head to tail, with razor sharp talons. Its eyes looked like black bullets about to be shot at me. It let out its ear-splitting shriek.' The way I described the rooster, I think readers could definitely imagine that scene." (See Figure 2–12.)

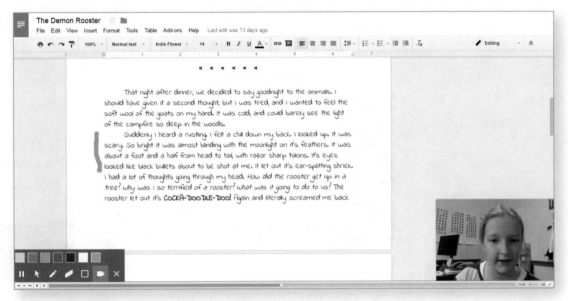

Figure 2–12 Molly's "Demon Rooster" Thoughtcast

- *When they're stuck or when something's not working:* Noticing
  something that seems off is critical for writers; even if we aren't
  sure of the solution, it gives us a pesky spot to return to when we're
  revising. It cues us that something else is needed, and our brains
  start to search for an alternative.

  For example, take Connor reflecting on his piece "Mushy Jack,"
  a poem of apology to the pumpkins he had smashed—gleefully—
  in his ten years of Halloweens. "I came up with this idea because
  when my class was thinking of poems and things we were sorry for,
  I thought of a jack-o'-lantern, because when it starts to rot, I kind of
  demolish them," Connor said, sounding not a bit apologetic in his
  thoughtcast.

  With typical fifth-grade humor, he shared some of his favorite
  lines of pumpkin carving and destruction—"I'm sorry / for cutting
  off your head / . . . for taking your brain / . . . for cutting out your
  eyes / . . . for stomping on you"—but also his struggles with writing
  the poem. By pausing and thinking metacognitively, he realized
  he needed to reorganize the poem so the lines made more sense.
  "I didn't really have [the lines] in the right [order]. I had 'taking
  out your brain'"—removing the jack-o'-lantern's seeds—"which is
  practically the first step, *after* 'letting you rot.' . . . I needed to revise
  it by moving stuff around." (See Figure 2–13.)

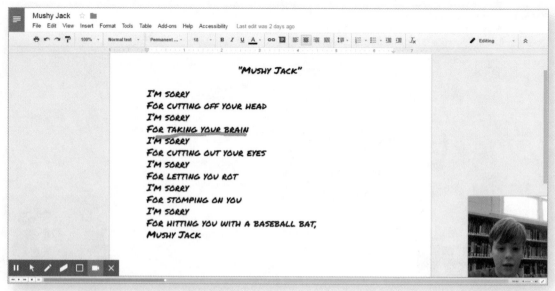

Figure 2–13 Connor's "Mushy Jack" Thoughtcast

With thoughtcasts like these, our students get in touch with the decisions they are making as writers. It also allows us, as teachers, to peer into their hearts and minds as they're crafting their drafts.

Practice: Revising Using Mindful Margins

For a low-tech variation on a thoughtcast, have your students take a draft and simply paste it onto a larger sheet, so they have a wide blank border to work with. Again, try this middraft, before their writing starts to feel done (and their thinking about it begins to ossify). Have your students describe their reflections about the piece—the revision moves they've tried, those they're still working on, successes, struggles, and uncertainties—right there in the margins, alongside their writing. Use the questions in Figure 2–7 (or ones you choose) and have your writers annotate by hand, all around the edges of their text.

Belief: Getting Meta Helps Writers Reflect on Our Stances

Metacognition makes us conscious of our decisions and reactions on a particular piece of writing but, perhaps more importantly, it makes us aware of our stances in general. It nudges us to look back not just at the page but at ourselves, to

consider how we're doing with each of these stances of a writer's mindset—optimism, perspective-taking, flexible thinking, transfer, and risk-taking.

When we're reflecting on a positive, generative line we've written—wondering, "What do I love about this? How can I build off it?"—we're getting meta, but we're also reflecting on our *optimism* and *persistence*. When we're reviewing a troublesome section of a draft and weighing different options—"What else could I try here?"—we're also considering our *flexible thinking*. When we

imagine what our potential readers might think about a certain section of text—"Would this part be clear to someone else?"—we are also shedding light on our *perspective-taking* and connection with our audience. On it goes.

Metacognition is so central to developing a writer's mindset because it allows us to reflect not just on a specific draft but on our "stance on the stances."

Practice: Setting Up Your Workshop with Writing Selfies

A writing selfie is a literary self-portrait in which students share their personal history with writing—their most indelible writing pieces and especially their process. Selfies can include students' earliest memories of writing right up to the present, including both the positive and the painful. A selfie can take many forms—a letter, a series of vignettes, a collection of images with captions. Whatever the form, have your students share their feelings about their most notable writing assignments; what they value and see as most important with writing; what they've learned about the qualities of good writing; what's challenging about writing; and more.

Selfies are great at the beginning of the year (when we're getting to know our writers and setting up our workshop) because they kick-start students' metacognition about their writing and about themselves as writers. It also gives us, as teachers, insight into each student's stances and the overall writing mindset they arrive with on day one.

Through their selfies, ask students to share the following:

- *What inspires them to write or what they enjoy about writing:* "I love to write because it's creative and fun," Kate said in her selfie. "When I write I can see it all in my mind. Words flow and my brain moves like it's a movie! I know what the characters will act like, how they will talk, and what they will say." Other students, like Abby, mentioned how certain settings, like the outdoors, spark their writing: "Sometimes when me and my sister are together we ride our bikes up to the top of our circle and bring clipboards and paper. There are trees at the top of the circle and we climb them and write in the trees."

  Others who struggle with some aspects of writing tap into the positive parts of the process through their selfie. "I like freewriting time, but I especially love to draw and doodle," Carter wrote. "I have five drawing journals. You should see them!" Hearing about his love of drawing helped me to work with Carter, who sometimes complained of having no ideas to write about. Thinking back on his selfie, I could remind him when he was feeling stuck that he had a rich resource he could pull from: the ideas sketched in his journals.

- *Their successes and sources of pride with writing:* For Will, it was a poem he wrote in second grade that made him think of himself as a writer for the first time. "I was sitting outside staring at a brick wall watching the bugs crawling along their merry way when I realized I was staring at what I was going to write. I got to it, writing whatever I saw—about how big and mighty the wall was protecting us from the weather, but also how the cracks in it gave the ants a route to wherever they were going. After, Mrs. Jones said it was one of the best poems she ever read. That was a lot of praise for a seven-year-old kid." (See Figure 2–14.)

- *What makes writing hard or frustrating for them:* We often learn about students who have felt defeated by writing, like Julia and Henry. "Everything I wrote [in the past] was a really bad piece of writing," Henry said. "Every single time I try to write, nothing comes to me. I just can't think. I'm not sure how to begin. I can't really write, I can only draw." It was clear Henry struggled with writing from our very first days together, but his selfie gave me some ideas about the root of the problem (initiating writing) and a starting place for interventions to try (introducing different types of brainstorming, scribing for him, using speech-to-text tools, and more).

    Julia's selfie provided more questions than answers but pointed to a difficult past with writing. "Dear Mr. Hall: As a writer I felt like a wimp. . . . In kindergarten and first grade I was the one who had trouble. In second and third grade I was struggling and had horrible handwriting. In fourth grade my teacher and parents helped me get through." I wondered, "What does she mean by 'a wimp'—that she gives up easily or can't generate lots of writing? What does she think qualifies some writing as good—and is she confusing presentation ('horrible handwriting') with content? What turned the corner for Julia last year?" Thinking about these questions would be important as I considered how I would confer with Julia in the year ahead. (See Figure 2–15).

Figure 2–14   Will's Writing Selfie

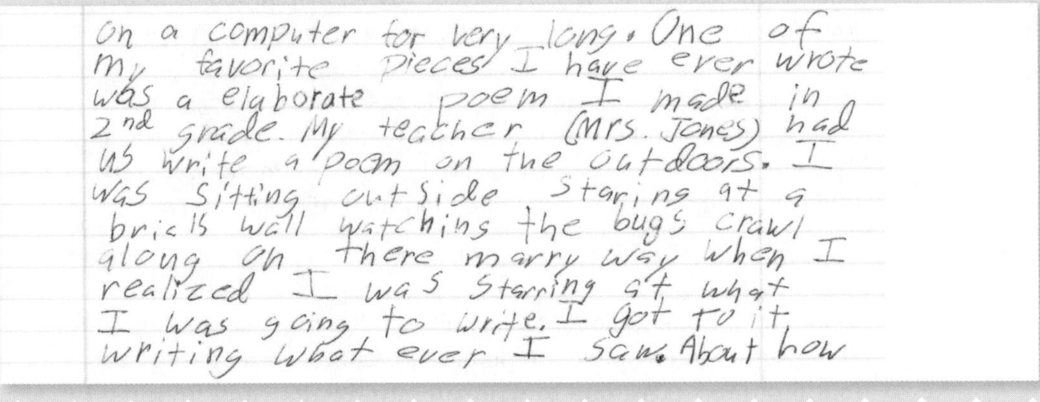

On a computer for very long. One of my favorite pieces I have ever wrote was a elaborate poem I made in 2nd grade. My teacher (Mrs. Jones) had us write a poem on the outdoors. I was sitting outside staring at a brick wall watching the bugs crawl along on there marry way when I realized I was staring at what I was going to write. I got to it writing what ever I saw. About how

Figure 2–15   Julia's Writing Selfie

Me as a writer

Dear mr.hall as a writer i felt like a wimp. I felt like i was proud for once last year. I always made my poems but they were bad. My parents and teachers helped me get through last year. I was discouraged and struggled last year. I was very bad at writing.

Figure 2–16   Melanie's Writing Selfie

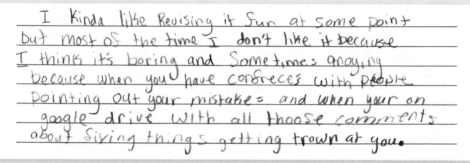

I Kinda like Revising it fun at some point but most of the time I don't like it because I think it's boring and Sometimes anaying because when you have corbreces with people Pointing out your mistakes and when your on google drive with all thoose comments about fixing things getting trown at you.

- *What helps them as writers and what doesn't:* "Sometimes I create great characters but there's no plot for them to be in," Kate offered. "When I get writer's block, it's major! For me, I need inspiration. . . . I need to know what type of story I will write. Will it be mystery? Adventure? Fiction? It helps me when I'm given parameters, like assigning a genre to write in. I just need something." Others, like Melanie, vented about what wasn't helpful or constructive for her. It's "annoying," she said, "when you're on Google Drive with all those comments about fixing things getting thrown at you." (See Figure 2–16.)

- *The craft moves and revision strategies they've learned and used before:* Cayden remembered a personal narrative he had written about a hike up Mount Washington, the highest peak in New Hampshire, and a specific type of lead embraced by many third and fourth graders. "We had to write an introduction, and for mine I put in a sound effect. I thought of the river you walk next to on the Ammonoosuc Trail, and I used the sound I heard the water making: 'wwwsshhh.'" Maryellen wrote about being taught how to insert ideas into a draft. "You can use a 'caret symbol' to add more in a place [where] there is no room and it looks like this: ∨ or ∧."

- *The messages about writing and revision that their past teachers (and parents) have instilled in them—whether positive or counter-productive:* Selfies give students an invitation to share the writing advice they've been given. Sometimes the advice is helpful and straightforward, like what Katie recalled hearing from one elementary teacher: "Read over your writing to check if it makes sense."

  Other messages students have internalized might run counter to the ones you are hoping to teach them. This was the case with Cayden when he kept adding more and more to his Mount Washington story. "When I thought I had finished, I wasn't, because my teacher told me to add *everything* on that trip. . . . I kept writing more paragraphs about going to Polly's Pancakes and the stores in North Conway." Though I hadn't read Cayden's story from the year before, I was fairly certain he should have been focusing more on the hike itself—which was most meaningful to him—rather than heaping on description about his breakfast or the side trip to L. L. Bean.

Through their selfies, we get a glimpse into our students' histories with writing—what they bring with them the moment they first walk through our classroom doors. Most importantly, selfies give our students a chance to practice metacognition by reflecting on their writing lives.

Practice: Reflecting Metacognitively on the Stances Through Minilessons

Each upcoming chapter in this book is dedicated to fostering one of the stances in a writer's mindset, and metacognition plays an integral part in each. In the chapters that follow—on optimism, perspective-taking, flexible thinking, transfer, and risk-taking—there are practices that are fueled by metacognition. Think of the stances as a network—the different nerve centers of a writer's mindset—with metacognition as the synapses connecting it all.

Here's a preview of some of the activities you will find:

- *Minilessons to find lines that tug at our pen:* Students reflect meta-cognitively about the most promising lines from their earliest drafts as a way to build off their strengths (from Chapter 3: "Optimism").

- *Minilessons to map a reader's reactions:* Students step into a reader's shoes and use their metacognitive skills to imagine that reader's reactions to their piece (from Chapter 4: "Perspective-Taking").

- *Minilessons to stretch our draft—and ourselves:* By thinking metacognitively about their draft and asking a series of "I wonder?" and "What if?" questions, writers stay open to new possibilities (from Chapter 5: "Flexible Thinking").

Belief: A Little Meta Goes a Long Way

There's a caveat in all this noticing and naming: the potential to kill the thing we love by overanalyzing it. (See Figure 2–17.) *Blinding flash:* extensive metacognition is *not* a preferred activity for most elementary and middle school students. It requires kids to pause, reread, slow down, and reflect—and we can overdo it if we're not careful.

Consider a read-aloud where the teacher stops constantly to draw out every possible interpretation, belaboring every teaching point and moving at a glacial pace (student groans and rolled eyes be damned). We want our students to be aware of their moves as writers, but we don't want them navel-gazing or constantly self-assessing and never moving forward, paralyzed by their inner critics.

Practice: Sprinkling Brief Meta Bursts Throughout Your Workshop

Getting meta—but not overdoing it—requires us to strike a balance during our writing workshop. Be judicious about when to ask students to reflect on their writing moves and when to simply stay immersed in drafting. Keep the tips in Figure 2–18 in mind.

Figure 2–17   Vivian's Reflection About Overdoing Revision

How do you feel about revising? Do you like to revise your writing? Why or why not?

I like revising except when you do it about 10 times a week.

Striking a Balance with Metacognition

▶ *Avoid extensive metacognition too early in the writing process* (other than perhaps to identify positives). If we ask ourselves, "Is this any good?" when we are first prewriting or drafting, the answer will likely be "No! What were you even thinking?!" and we'll abandon our writing before we've hardly begun.

▶ *Don't wait until after "The End."* If writers wait too long to shine a spotlight back on their writing, we may get overly attached and have a hard time letting go, changing, or being open to new ideas.

▶ *Strive for a mix of diving in and stepping back.* When we're asking students to think metacognitively, we're showing them how to step back and reflect—to consider where they are and what might come next in a draft. This step back is an important move—the focus of this chapter, obviously—but we shouldn't overuse it. For much of our time with students, we want them fully immersed, absorbed and in the flow of the act of writing. We want them in the writing zone most of the time, not being continually interrupted by our reflection prompts.

▶ *Keep metacognitive activities brief, periodic, and playful.* The metacognitive activities here (and in the following chapters) are a menu to choose from, not a checklist to complete. Use perhaps one meta activity per draft. Vary them up to keep things fresh. Try short bursts of metacognition with your students to keep it engaging.

Figure 2–18   Striking a Balance with Metacognition

Chapter

3

Optimism

Writers Develop by Building from Strengths

Will's optimism reared its head just as he was smashing an intruder's skull with a battle ax.

It was springtime and I was conferring with Will, who was deeply immersed in writing a fantasy-adventure piece called "Days of Red," a draft inspired by his love of the Ranger's Apprentice and The Lord of the Rings series. He was several chapters in and hard at work capturing the details of the grisly action—a clash between the heroes (three brothers, with the same names as his own siblings) and the Kalkara, a horde of seven-foot marauders laying siege to the walled city. Will had described several vivid scenes: the invading troops in their red armor breaking through the fog. Their wooden siege machines, pulled by oxen, being wheeled toward the wall. The defending archers, outnumbered, coating their arrows in oil and lighting them, hoping to stop the onslaught.

As he was revising, Will was adding more detail to the battle scenes, but he was most excited about the ways in which he was bringing his characters alive. "I'm trying to add more dialogue between the brothers and the other men," he told me. "I want to show what each one is like and how they act together—when they're arguing like brothers even as they're fighting the enemy."

Through the snippets of conversation he was adding, Will was giving shape to his heroes' personalities and relationships. There was their brotherly teasing and bickering in the early-morning moments just before the siege ("'Could you have slept any longer?' Dan mumbled as he rolled his eyes at Will. 'We have bigger problems than your beauty sleep.'"). There was their fearlessness mixed with humor ("'Die, you fleshless sack maggot!'"). There was the thirst for battle among all the soldiers ("'Let's cut these mangy dogs down to size.'").

These bits of dialogue were drawing Will back into his piece—into the hard work of revising it. This is optimism as I mean it: a magnet that draws our eyes and ears toward the best lines we've written. Optimism pulls us toward the ideas with the most potential.

When it comes to a writer's mindset, optimism isn't a sunny disposition, blind positivity, or an imperviousness to the frustrations of revision. Just the opposite. It's having a clear-eyed acknowledgment of all the challenges revision poses—and then taking them on anyway *because our draft is worth it*.

Students may grouse about the difficulties of revising. This was true with Will, who started the year making it clear he wasn't fond of reworking his drafts or open to ideas about changing them. "I don't like revising because it bores me to death and in [my] opinion is very hard," he had written in his September survey (see Figure 3–1).

But over time as we kept experimenting with our drafts, Will's perception of revision began to soften. His first drafts—pieces about driving on his grandfather's tractor and going clamming with his dad—transformed in unexpected ways. He refashioned narratives into poems. He started to see conferences with teachers and classmates as helpful conversations, as opposed to directives being imposed on him. In late spring, while he was in the thick of crafting "Days of Red," he paused to reflect on how far he had come. "At the beginning of the year, I was so-so with revision; I didn't like it, but I didn't hate it," Will said, in a bit of revisionist history (He *hated* it!). "As the year has progressed, I have gotten to like it more and more. Mostly because it makes my story better, more exciting, and breathtaking." (See Figure 3–2.)

Figure 3–1   Will's First Survey

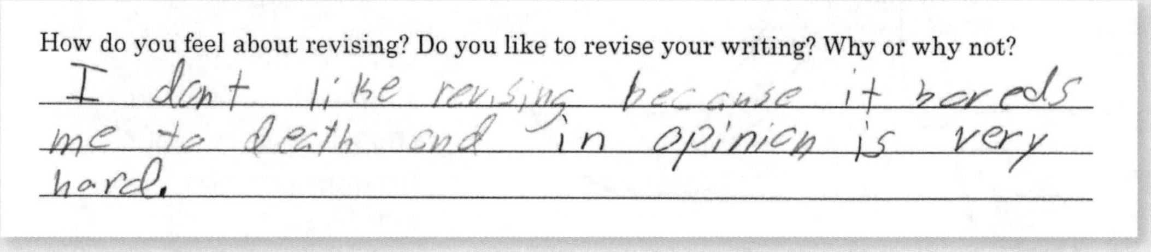

How do you feel about revising? Do you like to revise your writing? Why or why not?

I dont like revising because it bords me to death and in opinion is very hard.

Figure 3–2   Will's End-of-Year Survey

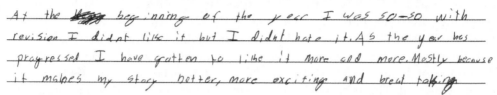

How do you feel about revising? Do you like to revise your writing? Why or why not?

At the ~~begin~~ beginning of the year I was so-so with revision I did't like it but I did't hate it. As the year has progressed I have gotten to like it more and more. Mostly because it makes my story better, more exciting and breat taking

Optimism isn't falling in love with every phrase we put to the page. It's the noticing—and building off of—the ideas we've written that are most striking to us. It's finding the lines that keep us going and feeling positive. It's caring so much about a piece of writing that we just have to get the words right. (See Figure 3–3.)

Looking over my quickwrite, which lines stand out? Which ones tug at my pen?

This—right here—seems like the heart of my piece. That's the idea I want to focus on.

My readers loved this part. Maybe I could build off it . . .

Out of all the brainstormed ideas I could choose, this is the one I'm most psyched to try . . .

Figure 3–3   Optimism

Belief: Students Should Learn to Build from Their Strengths

Optimism with writing came late for me. I arrived at college as a lukewarm writer, someone with a few positive experiences but mostly stifled by the need to get my words down perfectly. When I was younger, I watched in awe as other elementary and middle school classmates seemed to pluck wonderful stories and poems from the ether. Years later, I would wait for the ideal thesis statement to emerge for an essay, stalled like a frozen chess player over a board, trying to envision every step before making a move.

That is, until my Freshman English teacher, Bruce Ballenger (1990), gave us "permission to write badly," showing us how to write as fast as possible, how to outrun our internal critics. Deeply influenced by his mentor, Don Murray, Ballenger gave us a host of ways to plunge into a draft, such as freewriting, brainstorming, and "clustering," or webbing—commonplace now but revolutionary to me then. We wrote every day, filling our journals, understanding

Figure 3–4   Momo Shows Optimism About His Work

Figure 3–5 Keira Writes with Excitement

that some lines would be humdrum but that others would hold promise. We circled surprises—unexpected, generative lines or ideas we had written—as a way to discover what we were trying to say, a way to figure out "what we didn't know we knew." I suddenly found my words rushing out. I found my voice, my stories.

It may seem counterintuitive, but we can bolster our students' optimism by giving them permission to "write badly." We can help them develop a writer's Teflon—a sense that the dreary, stale words we sometimes (*OK*, often) produce don't stick to us. By asking our students to write in frequent, brief bursts—and making a habit of this, generating volume—we can lower the stakes and take the pressure off any one particular piece. By having students start *lots* of potential pieces, we give them a range of options so they can identify the most promising and build on them.

Practice: Prewriting to Free Us from Our Internal Critics

We need to show students prewriting approaches that allow them to silence their inner critics (or at least quiet them down). When prewriting with your students, the goal is to generate lots of possibilities and identify those with the most potential. Try a variety of approaches, such as those in Figure 3–6.

Whatever prewriting approaches you use with your students, remember the following tips:

- *Be explicit with students about the purpose.* Tell them the goal is to produce lots of ideas—and to suspend judgment on them for now. Remind them to live in limbo, keep an open mind, and avoid the rush to choose one idea.

- *De-emphasize grammar, conventions, and mechanics.* Conventions can help us make our ideas easier to read and understand, but don't allow these to slow students down.

Prewriting to Free Us from Our Internal Critics

▶ *Quickwriting:* **Have students write for five minutes or so in response to a mentor text (provide examples from published authors *and* former students). Find book excerpts that are evocative and will connect with your students. Encourage students to "borrow a line" from the text and riff off it—letting the line guide their thinking (Rief 2014, 4).**

▶ *Webbing and listing:* **Sometimes the best way to get initial writing ideas out—and to circumvent our inner censors—is through webbing (sometimes called mind mapping) or listing, since these don't require full sentences or complete ideas. I often use webs and lists when we're first brainstorming (e.g., "Times I Was Afraid," "Family Stories," or "Injuries and Accidents"), as a way to spark lots of possibilities or as a precursor to diving into a quickwrite.**

▶ *Visual strategies:* **When the author Jack Gantos visited our school years ago, he regaled us with bizarre, riveting stories of his childhood—all of which sprung from annotated maps he had drawn of his home and neighborhood in Florida. These were not your typical maps; they included items such as a broken arm, an exploding hot dog, his pet cockroach, and a crushed bike, and they were rich with seeds of potential writing. I often use visuals like these—memory maps—to get my students thinking about their own stories. Visual strategies give students another way to stockpile writing ideas quickly, bypass their internal writing judge, and create a sense of optimism. (See Figure 3–7.)**

Figure 3–6   Prewriting to Free Us from Our Internal Critics

- *Give lots of prewriting practice*—perhaps five to ten different sessions, or minibursts—*before asking your students to choose one* to revise.

- *Keep sessions brief and frequent.*

- *Have a way for students to collect these prewrites* (we use a reader's-writer's journal and a writing folder).

- *Establish realistic expectations* and highlight the power of the writing routine. Tell them: "Some days we'll have dry spells—duds—but other days we'll be teeming with writing and ideas. The key is to keep up the habit."

Figure 3–7 Visual prewriting strategies—including neighborhood maps, life graphs, identity webs, and heart maps—give students another way to generate writing ideas, building a sense of optimism.

Practice: Using Minilessons to Model Building Off Our Strengths

As writers, we are often our own toughest critics, harboring those voices that hide in a corner of our brains—or sit up front and center—telling us our writing's no good. That we should give it up—sometimes before we've hardly begun. For this reason, it's important that our students periodically reflect on what's working well in their own writing.

Find Lines That Tug at Our Pen

When Cooper began a quickwrite in the fall, he started by focusing on his struggles with writing—his difficulties with finding story ideas and especially feeling plagued by editing and "typos":

> Typos are a common thing in writing that you are almost guaranteed to make. Typos are a miss spelt [*sic*] word or phrase that you will often see in a story and if you say you don't make typos, you are lying to yourself and the world. You may or may not see typos in this piece already but trust me, I have made plenty!

Ironically, Cooper found lines he loved in a piece about his own writing blunders. Taking a few moments to consider what was working—his honesty, voice, and sense of humor—gave him an unexpected boost and a desire to keep going. Cooper decided to revise this piece, reflecting on other writing foibles. What he ended up creating was a playful confessional and handbook rolled into one.

Make it a habit to have your students hunt for hidden gems in their writing, especially in their earliest drafts, when optimism is often at its most tenuous.

Figure 3–9 outlines a process for mining our writing.

Figure 3–8   Ben Looks for a Favorite Line

Find Lines That Tug at Our Pen

Ask your writers to reread their quickwrites, brainstorms, lists, and first drafts and then follow these steps:

1. Highlight, underline, or star a favorite line or section they've written.

2. Jot a note in the margin (or just reflect silently) about *why* this part seemed powerful or energizing.

3. Reflect briefly about *what they noticed* in their writing (e.g., a craft move; an unexpected memory; a line reminding them of a favorite author's).

4. Share the line with a partner or small group.

5. Perhaps try beginning the following day's writing workshop with this line or section. Tell them to let this favorite part lead their thinking and writing.

Figure 3–9   Find Lines That Tug at Our Pen

Model how to build on strengths

It helps to show students how writers begin to construct a draft from a few promising lines. As teachers, we can model optimism by sharing our writing, honing in on the parts that tug at our pens and inspire us to continue. See Figure 3–10 for ideas on how to model this for your students.

Seeing you, their teacher, sharing your draft—and the origins of your own optimism—helps demystify the writing process for students. It shows them how we parlay our initial positivity into concrete revisions. Here are some suggestions for sharing:

- Project your draft with a document camera or an interactive whiteboard, or give students a copy (so they can see the specific lines you're responding to).

- Read parts of your draft out loud, pausing in places to think aloud.

- Discuss *what* you noticed (the specific lines, ideas, or aspects you liked), *why* these struck you, and *how* you plan to build off these.

- Use this modeling before you kick off a writing session, or after, as part of an end-of-period share.

- When you're done, invite students to consider ways they have used these same moves in the past—or how they might use them in a current piece.

Model How to Build on Strengths

Here are three modeling strategies to try.

▶ *Build off exciting, generative lines.*

Show how some parts stand out—perhaps because of the sound of the words, the vividness of a phrase, the emotions they evoke, or a craft move you've made (even unconsciously). Show how your excitement for this part can spur new ideas and lines. Here's an example I've shared with students:

> "In my Colonial diary entry, I'm trying to write from the perspective of a kid sailing on the *Mayflower*. I wrote these lines about the sounds on board—'I hear the waves slapping against the ship's hull . . . the anxious bleating of the sheep below deck'—and I'm getting fired up to add more things I could hear. I could add the noise of the wind from a storm, the hymns the Pilgrims sang to calm their nerves—and, yes, even the retching of people getting seasick. I bet I could add details using other senses, too—like what I could feel, smell . . ."

▶ *Identify lines that trigger a positive response in readers.*

If you've shared a draft of your piece and received some positive reactions, share how these motivate you to keep revising.

> "I'm writing about this time when my dog, who's a terrier, flipped out—at 3:00 a.m., of course—when she smelled a skunk outside. We had guests in our house, and there was a mad dash with me trying to chase her down in the dark to keep her from waking up the whole neighborhood. I shared the writing with my daughter this morning, and she laughed out loud in a few places, like 'The furry white blur catapults off the edge of the

Figure 3–10   Model How to Build on Strengths   *(continues)*

bed and hits the floor at a sprint. It sputters and snarls, bursts in wild figure eights around the room. I whip my body up in an awkward cartwheel—one leg caught in the bedspread—hopping in pursuit.' It was great hearing my daughter crack up over this story! She said she loved how this was like a slapstick, slow-motion movie scene in her mind. That made me want to find another place in the draft where I could stretch out the moment and exaggerate my reactions for another laugh."

▶ *Follow an unexpected turn or discovery.*

Show how to identify when a draft takes a surprising turn—and how to go where it takes you.

"I started this piece as a sports memory—playing floor hockey in the family room with my stepdad when I was in sixth grade. (I know, I know: you shouldn't take a slap shot with a tennis ball inside your house!) As I'm rereading this part, though, I'm thinking what it's really about isn't our crazy hockey matches but our strained relationship. I'm realizing that these impromptu hockey showdowns were one of the only times my stepfather and I spent any time together, just us. I think I'll write more about this and some of the ways we didn't see eye to eye."

Practice: Conferring and Peer Conferring Around Strengths

Dedicate some conferences to simply focusing on what's working with your students' writing—the knock-the-ball-out-of-the-park successes and even just the promising attempts and the "almost said." Stay laser focused on the positives of a piece and avoid the temptation to stray off into the *but*s ("This piece has a great lead, *but* . . .").

We can certainly set aside times for critical feedback, but when we're trying to build optimism—particularly early in the life of a draft—it helps to cast a spotlight on its potential, not its shortcomings.

Try "kudos only" with peers

When you have your students give each other writing feedback, ask them periodically to limit it to "kudos only." For a variety of reasons, some students may resist this, so front-load it with a brief class discussion.

- Discuss *why* we might want to focus solely on the strengths in each other's drafts (e.g., it keeps us writing, especially early in the process, when we're not quite ready for suggestions).

- Discuss *how* to give meaningful praise by being specific. Ask your class: "How would pointing out *specific* lines or strengths of a piece be helpful?" (e.g., so the writer would know exactly what worked; so they could try similar lines or moves in other sections or future drafts).

- Encourage readers to point out strengths—genuine ones—even if a piece seems rough at first. Show them how to comment on the promising ideas that seem important (even if they aren't fully realized yet). Model how they can praise the writer's efforts (for example, an *attempt* to use a craft move, like dialogue), even if they fall a bit short.

Figure 3–11 shares some tips for how to focus on strengths during conferences.

To get your students to focus on strengths, you could use a version of the Peer Conference Kudos handout (see Figure 3–12) or try any number of creative variations. One of my students, Courtney, asked to create a "poetry pocket" for each student in our class—a little pouch where we could slip positive notes about each other's writing to one another. (See Figure 3–13.)

Single Out Strengths

Whether it's you, the teacher, conferring with students, or you're asking them to confer with each other, center on the following during your conversations:

▶ *Identify lines that struck you or stayed with you* **for some reason. What sticks in your mind or resonates with you? What seemed memorable, powerful, or interesting? Point out these lines. (If you have your own copy, you might underline these lines; otherwise, you can write them on a half-sheet of paper.)**

▶ *Identify parts that seemed to have special importance or weight*—**even if they weren't the main points. Point out spots that seemed powerful to you—the sources of energy in the writing.**

▶ *Share why these lines seemed strong.* **Jot down reasons why these lines stood out. What thoughts or feelings did they evoke in you as a listener? If possible, point out places where the writer may have used similar craft moves to those in mentor texts you've read together.**

Adapted from Peter Elbow and Pat Belanoff's Pointing and Center of Gravity technique (1995, 8–9).

Figure 3–11   Single Out Strengths

Throughout the week, we would take time to read new poems from our peers posted on the bulletin board and then leave each other praise.

In her note to River about his piece "Swamp Shoes," Olivia pointed out the personification he was using ("I like how you act like the shoes are people"). (See Figure 3–14.) She also noticed—and relished—how he had apologized to his shoes for destroying them with his "smelly toes" and "sweaty heels." Olivia's comment was a nod to the apology poems we had read in class (including William Carlos Williams' classic "This Is Just to Say"); in this way, she had connected River's efforts to a mentor text we had all read (and loved).

Peer Conference Kudos

Writer's Name:_____

Title of Writing Piece:_____

Response from:_____

Date:_____

Reminders:

- Focus on strengths and potential in the draft.
- Be specific, positive, and honest.

What lines, sections, or ideas stood out or stuck with you? (For example, "The lines that stand out to me are . . ." or "The part that struck me was . . .")

What did you notice about these lines, sections, or ideas? Why did they seem strong, powerful, or memorable? (For example, "I noticed . . ."; "This part made me feel . . ./think about . . . as a reader"; "You did a strong job with [specific writing skill or craft move]"; "I could tell you put effort into . . .")

Figure 3–12   Peer Conference Kudos Handout

Belief: Students Should Choose What to Write and Revise

"Sometimes, everything in school feels like an obligation," Molly, an eighth grader, proclaimed.

Autumn, sitting nearby, agreed. "It helps to have freedom with what I can write—to not have a lot of 'borders' or strict guidelines. I don't need a completely blank canvas, but I don't want to feel like I'm following a rulebook with my writing."

For students to be optimistic and persistent with their writing, they need to own it. We can't spark authentic revision or develop a writer's mindset in our students unless they have plenty of *choice*—choice in writing topics, genre, audience, what to add and take out, and more.

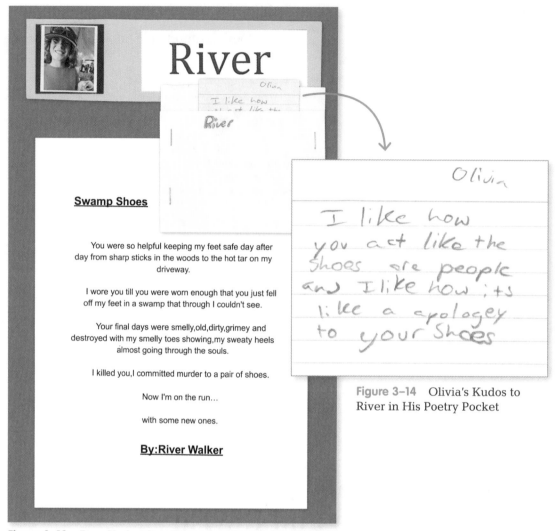

Swamp Shoes

You were so helpful keeping my feet safe day after day from sharp sticks in the woods to the hot tar on my driveway.

I wore you till you were worn enough that you just fell off my feet in a swamp that through I couldn't see.

Your final days were smelly,old,dirty,grimey and destroyed with my smelly toes showing,my sweaty heels almost going through the souls.

I killed you,I committed murder to a pair of shoes.

Now I'm on the run...

with some new ones.

By:River Walker

Olivia

I like how you act like the shoes are people and I like how its like a apology to your shoes

Figure 3–14   Olivia's Kudos to River in His Poetry Pocket

Figure 3–13   Peer Kudos Can Take Many Forms

This probably isn't an earth-shattering concept for you. But we can all use a reminder from time to time that when our students aren't excited or invested in their writing, it may be that *they don't feel it's theirs.*

It can be hard for us as teachers to make the shift from writing we choose for children to writing they choose for themselves. I'd love to say I've done this naturally and easily, but the truth is, it's been tough for me let go of the reins. When I tried full choice years ago, sometimes my workshop felt out of control. My students would be immersed in such a wide variety of genres and topics that I often had a hard time keeping it all straight. I wondered how I would choose minilessons to teach or help them in conferences, with every writer veering off in such different directions. What rubric would we use? How would I grade their work? Sometimes the choices they made—convoluted fantasy stories that seemed to go on and on—made me groan.

With all of these obstacles to individual choice, I tended to play it safe. I picked a genre for us to focus on (say, memoir in the fall or poetry in the spring), allowed students to choose from a range of content, and made peace with it. The kids had their choice of topics; *wasn't that enough?*

The problem was, those parameters could feel like confines. My belief in choice nagged at me.

So, perhaps like many of you, I'm still working at transitioning to greater student choice. There *are* times when our class writing looks similar—because of common experiences I want my students to have, tasks my school requires, or standards I have to address—but I'm committing myself to handing off as much control and autonomy as I can.

Practice: Setting Up Your Writing Workshop to Expand Student Choice

As you set up your writing workshop—at the beginning and throughout the year—try the following to build in as much choice as possible.

Have students brainstorm different entry points for choice writing.

Throughout the fall, I have students develop running lists of writing possibilities. With each of the lists, I model my own for the class first. Then, after students have a crack at it, I ask them to share their emerging ideas in pairs, in table groups, or with the whole class. The point of sharing is to expand our lists by listening to others. I try different entry points—various invitations to get us writing—such as the ones in Figure 3–15.

Entry Points for Choice Writing

▸ **Content:** *What is important to you? What do you care about?* **We brainstorm lists of topics that matter to us—indelible memories, people and places that are special to us, hobbies that sustain us, issues we care about. As a class, we discuss content categories—the "stuff" writing can be about (sports, friends, fears, accomplishments, painful memories, joyful moments)—and from there we generate detailed lists.**

▸ **Purpose:** *Why do we write?* **Ask students to list as many real reasons for writing as they can think of (see Figure 3–16). "To write a love letter— make somebody fall in love with you," Dylan says, which draws laughs from his classmates, but he's right. Our students often surprise us with the authentic purposes they think of:** *To entertain. To make someone feel what we feel. To vent. Because we have a story in our head we want out. Stress relief. To get something off your chest. To save a fragment of ourselves. To make a difference.* **We often start with topics, but** *purpose* **is what really fuels us as writers. There's a social media post gnawing at us that we just have to respond to. A letter we're compelled to write to sway the school board. An email we type into the wee hours to reconnect with a distant friend.**

   Ask your students to pick a purpose from their list (e.g., "To persuade someone") and flesh it out in detail. "What do you feel strongly about? Whom would you try to persuade—and what would you convince them of?"

▸ **Genre:** *What are all the different types of writing we can do? What are some that are comfortable and familiar—your go-to genres? Which are new or unusual to you? Which might you try?* **If we're going to try to blow up genre-based writing units, we need students to have an idea of all the options they have. When students begin listing all the genres they know, it often starts slowly and generally—fiction, poems, fantasy—but it doesn't take long for them to come up with surprising, inventive ideas.** *Food review. Graphic novel. Fable. Movie script. Greek myth. Obituary.* **Their list can be a starting place, and as students decide to dive into new territory, we can help by finding mentor texts to explore the features of whatever genre they take on.**

▶ **Audience:** *Whom might you write to? Whom could your writing be useful to, or whom might it influence? Who might be interested in hearing it, or whom would you want to hear back from?* **Initially, students often come up short when you ask about audience; most simply haven't thought about it before. To be fair, we as educators don't usually** *ask them* **to think about it. The types of writing we often require are school assignments, with an audience of one (the teacher). But when we take time to brainstorm who our potential readers might be—***close friends, grandparents, kids from other schools, President Trump, our future self***—our words and ideas immediately start to bend toward that presence at the other end of our lines.**

Figure 3–15   Entry Points for Choice Writing

The entry points listed in Figure 3–15 work only if we allow students to use them. Throughout the year, I remind students to look back at their lists for writing ideas—topics, purposes, genre, audience—even as I'm guiding them in other aspects of their writing.

Unite around a purpose

It's late September right now in my classroom, and my eighth graders are knee-deep in choice. Rose is writing a series of poetic vignettes showing the journey of a treasured blanket through a girl's life. Ulysses is focusing his entire memoir on a few seconds of penalty kicks at the end of a fateful soccer semifinal. Elsa is writing her own obituary. Amid this sea of genres, there is one guideline: to "share something important about yourself" with us. I've given this overarching purpose because (1) it's early in the school year and we don't

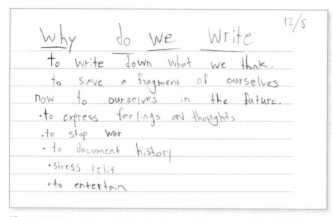

Figure 3–16 Henry's Brainstormed Purposes for Writing

> Why do we Write 12/5
> to write down what we think.
> to save a fragment of ourselves
> now to ourselves in the future.
> · to express feelings and thoughts
> · to stop war
> · to document history
> · stress relif
> · to entertain

know one another yet and (2) our school, in response to the coronavirus pandemic, is completely remote, and I'm desperate to build our class community. I presented students with several different mentor texts, we tried some quickwrites, but I allowed genre to run free. I've guided the purpose, but they are in control of what shape the writing will take.

Use craft and process studies

Other times, we can open up genre to students by having them take on a process or craft study. One of my colleagues, Emily Geltz, started experimenting with this after noticing the boost in her students' engagement when they had more choice, when they could *play*. "Come read our story about this guy who can't stop farting!" they squealed, giggling as she got to each instance of flatulence. She wanted this level of excitement and joy, but she knew some structure was needed to nudge her students' learning. After reading Matt Glover's *Craft and Process Studies* (2020), she decided to try units that centered on specific skills in process (such as revision or peer conferences) or craft (such as text structures or careful word choice). Emily decided to immerse her students in a process study of revision, which gave her a focus for her minilessons and feedback but also gave them freedom of choice (in genre and topic). A win-win (even if she had to read more about farts).

I'm structuring choice in similar ways. Like Emily, I'm trying more units that allow students freedom of genre and topic by focusing on craft moves that cut across genres. We work on powerful, vivid language (e.g., sensory details, specific word choice, figurative language, repetition, strong verbs). We study structures authors use to play with time (e.g., flashbacks, flashforwards, stretched-out moments). We hone our beginnings, endings, and titles (to engage and surprise, to leave readers with questions, to come full circle, to leave us with a feeling or insight). These and other craft lessons transcend genres and become my teaching frame during these choice units.

And yes, we can still teach genre-based units throughout the year. There is nothing wrong with a study of poetry, memoir, or persuasive writing, so long as we offer choice as much as we can.

Seek out resources

There are many books about how to make your writing workshop rich with student choice. I'm still reading—and rereading—them, striving to get a bit better each day, striving to stay a little truer to my belief in a student-centered classroom.

Here are a few helpful resources if you're looking to give students more control:

- *Craft and Process Studies*, by Matt Glover (2020). This book for K–6 classrooms (and beyond) shows how to break the bonds of genre-based units—how to allow students to choose their writing genre while still teaching important skills by focusing on authors' processes and craft moves.

- *Joy Write*, by Ralph Fletcher (2017). This short, compelling book is a call to increase student engagement by giving kids more choice, even letting them go "feral" (63).

- *Read Write Teach*, by Linda Rief (2014). Linda was my mentor when I was a student teacher, and this is an invaluable guidebook to her classroom. It's an in-depth invitation to how a veteran language arts teacher incorporates student voice and choice into the very bones of a workshop.

- *In the Middle*, by Nancie Atwell (1998). I periodically go back to this classic by the guru of middle school language arts. It's full of insights and practical ideas about weaving choice into our writing instruction.

- *Blending Genre, Altering Style*, by Tom Romano (2000). Romano opens your eyes to using multigenre projects with your students, allowing them to explore a topic using a range of writing forms.

Practice: Using Minilessons to Model Choice

Not every brainstormed idea *should* be written. Not every quickwrite and draft we begin *should* be revised. Drafting and revision demand so much of us, so only certain pieces should rise to this level. Show students how to identify those pieces that are worthy by trying minilessons like the ones in Figure 3–17.

Choosing What to Write and Revise

▸ *Discuss and reflect:* **Hold a brief class discussion: "Why would a writer choose one piece over another to start—or to revise?" List the reasons your students come up with on the board. These are some of my students' typical reasons for choosing an idea to draft or revise:**

- I remember this idea most vividly or clearly.
- I have the most to say about it.
- I'm most excited, interested, or energized as I think about this idea (or as I reread what I've written about it so far).
- It's the idea I care most deeply about, the one closest to my heart.
- It's about an important moment from my life.
- When I think about this idea, I react the most strongly (it's the most funny; scary; tense; jaw-dropping; painful; surprising).
- I'm curious about this idea and want to explore it further with my writing.

▸ *Use a writing smorgasbord:* **Model how you, as a teacher-writer, make choices. Pull out your recent prewrites and quickwrites from your journal or folder and lay them out in front of you and your students. Use a think-aloud to share your process for deciding which piece to draft or revise. "I know we've started a lot of narrative writing pieces these past few weeks—from times we were afraid, to scar stories, to joyful moments. Since I know I'm going to spend some time revising one of these, I want to choose carefully, so I'm going to take a few minutes to look over each of the pieces I've started. I'll skim over them to see which one I'm most excited about and which one brings up the strongest emotions."**

▸ *Declare your commitment:* **It's not exactly a betrothal, but when we commit to revising a piece of writing, it shouldn't be on impulse. The best choices aren't ones kids decide willy-nilly, but those they pick intentionally. John wrote about hitting a grand slam because "it was an important part of [his] life and there [was] a lot to write about." For Hayden, writing about a strange neighborhood dare—a group of friends eating hot peppers straight out of the garden—was an opportunity to "share all the emotions [they] were going through with the readers." (See Figure 3–18.)**

Figure 3–17 Choosing What to Write and Revise

Figure 3-18   Hayden's Predrafting Decision Sheet

Name: Hayden S.   Date:

Section:

Of all the ideas you brainstormed/quickwrote/listed, which one are you choosing? *(Share your draft idea in 1-2 sentences)*

The story I am choosing is when I lived at my old house our neighbors came over and we were playing in our backyard. Then all the sudden we got the urge to try the red hot peppers in our garden.

WHY are you choosing to turn this one into a draft? *(What makes you most excited about this idea? Explain in 1-2 sentences)*

What makes me most excited about this topic is that I get to share all the emotions we were going through with the readers.

Ask students to pause before jumping headlong into any revision by having them reflect on a half-sheet of paper: *Which piece have you decided to draft or revise? Why are you choosing this one?* Simply posing these questions is powerful. It underscores that students *have* a choice—and that whatever they select should matter deeply to them.

Practice: Conferring Around Choice

When talking with students about choosing, refocusing, or abandoning a draft, strive for quick conferences with students early in the drafting process to ask about their decision. *Why did they choose to revise the piece they did? Why is it important to them? Why are they sticking with it?* When I sat down next to Deepthi, a soft-spoken eighth grader writing a persuasive essay about the need to lower the voting age to sixteen, it was obvious she had reflected on her *why*. She told me lowering the voting age became important to her once she began reading articles about the Parkland High School survivors and their activism to curb gun violence. "I follow many of them on social media, and I found it really moving how they set up this entire event [March for our Lives]," she said. "I thought how they have a voice, too, and how they deserve to be heard. Some people think sixteen-year-olds aren't mature enough to vote, but I think they're more than mature enough."

Figure 3–19   Shreya and I Confer Around Her Writing Choices

Conferring with students about their choice can help them find their focus, the heart of their piece. When I spoke with Matt, who was writing about a vacation to Hawaii with his grandparents, he described his *why*: "I learned to surf for the first time, something I always wanted to try." But as we looked over his draft, he noticed he hadn't included surfing in his piece yet, and he was already on page 3. He had described the flight, his jetlag, and the impressive, lavish hotel, and, as we conferred, it dawned on him that his reason for writing was getting lost.

Sometimes writers might realize a piece isn't as significant to them as they thought. Or they start a piece and feel obligated to continue, even if their hearts aren't in it or their optimism is flagging.

This was the case with Alyssa, a talented writer whose draft was quite funny and already had some wonderful dialogue. As we conferred, though, it became obvious something was missing. "I'm writing about this time when I fell off one of the swings at the school playground when I was in first grade, but I'm not that into it. . . . It just didn't mean that much to me." We discussed the importance of paying attention to this feeling and allowing herself to let that piece go. By the end of the period, Alyssa had identified a different idea from her journal—a mortifying memory from her basketball season. "I sprained my ankle in the game, but more importantly, this was the moment when I really started to *hate* basketball. It was so *embarrassing*!"

Our conferences, like this one with Alyssa, can be a chance to destigmatize "draft dropping." Drafting and revising take significant time, energy, and attention, so we should be selective about what we choose, and we should change course—even abandon a draft—if we need to (so long as we're not doing it constantly).

Belief: When Teachers Do Decide, Keep It Real

The morning after our climate change night, my students were still buzzing. Over the past month, we had been working with faculty from our local university to learn the science behind our changing climate. The capstone to this project was an evening presentation in our library, with my fifth graders presenting their research to over one hundred family and community members. Their scripts—on the causes of climate change, its potential effects on our area in New Hampshire, steps we could take to make a positive impact—had been revised over and over (see Figure 3–20).

The following day at morning meeting, my students looked like athletes after a championship win. Their faces were a mix of relief, exhaustion, and mostly palpable pride. "What do you think helped you to do such a great job improving your scripts and presentations?" I asked.

"What helped me was having a real audience," Wilson said, and the heads around the circle started nodding.

"It helped us be more serious when we were writing and rehearsing when we realized people were *really* coming," Peter added.

We can keep our students more positive and persistent if the writing we do assign is meaningful—if it has an authentic purpose and audience. As teachers, it's important to be wary of almost-real writing— assignments that have

Figure 3–20   Kelly Presents at the Climate Change Night

a ring of veracity to them but turn out to be hollow. Will a film or restaurant review be published so that an audience can actually benefit from it, or will it exist only as an exercise? Will a science pamphlet that gets at informational writing skills be circulated, or will it only be handed in to the teacher?

Practice: Getting Real with the Writing You Assign

There are times when we are required to teach certain types of writing, or when we want to assign a common task to the whole class. Even when the writing is teacher-generated, consider the questions in Figure 3–21 to help your students stay more positive and persistent with it.

Try the following to hunt for ideas for genuine writing assignments:

- *Ask students what real writing they see a need for.* Several years ago when we were writing book reviews and posting them around our classroom, one of my students asked, "Why don't we have a display of our book reviews in the school library, so more kids will see them?" From that one student suggestion, our reviews suddenly burst out of our isolated corner of the hallway and were being read by the entire school. (See Figures 3–22 and 3–23.) My fifth graders saw their writing in the hands of students they had never met. Our librarian told them that their reviews were responsible for a notice-able surge in book checkouts. Listening to my students suddenly allowed me to provide a deeper purpose for our writing and revising.

Getting Real with the Writing You Assign

▶ Is the writing task authentic—does it exist in the world?

▶ Is there a compelling purpose for it?

▶ Is there an authentic reader—or lots of potential readers—on the other end of the lines your students will be writing?

▶ Where could their writing live? Where could their audience interact with it (e.g., a bulletin board, a blog, a public presentation)?

Figure 3–21 Getting Real with the Writing You Assign

Figure 3–22   Part of Our Summer Reading Book Review Display in Our School Library

Figure 3–23   Book Review for Ghost

- *Keep your eyes open to opportunities in your community.* A few years ago, our local estuary was everywhere in the news. The state utility company had decided to lay underground electric cables beneath its waters, and citizen activists became concerned that pollutants could be released into this fragile ecosystem.

  Reminded of the importance of Great Bay, we decided to raise awareness about all the ways it was special, ecologically and historically. We asked students to develop PSAs—public service announcements—about a topic related to the bay. (See Figures 3–24 and 3–25.) Some wrote about key species (such as eelgrass, oysters, or osprey). Others researched the history of the bay, including an event in the 1970s when town members rose up and thwarted a proposed oil refinery on its shores. Some students wrote about our waste and how it affects the bay's water quality (with the memorable subtitle, "What's in Your Pee and Does It Really Go in Great Bay?"). When opportunities like this arise and we take them on, our students know their writing matters.

- *Consider ways to expand your audience.* One of my eighth-grade colleagues recently turned me on to the Global Read Aloud, a K–12 project that connects students across the world as they craft

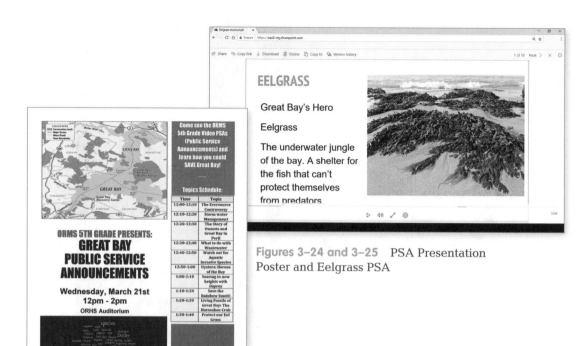

Figures 3–24 and 3–25   PSA Presentation
Poster and Eelgrass PSA

responses to a common book. Students share their reactions, questions, predictions, and observations with a global audience through online tools such as Skype, Padlet, and Flipgrid. From the moment my New Hampshire public school students watched the videos sent to us by a class from New Zealand—each student wearing a school uniform and speaking in a thick Kiwi accent—the project suddenly shifted. Our own reading responses—which they wrote and revised first, then recorded—suddenly had real meaning.

- *Look across subject areas.* When we were learning about the precursors to the American Revolution in social studies, we made plans to visit nearby Boston—a hotbed of Colonial unrest—and its Freedom Trail. We decided to flip the usual paradigm—teacher as tour guide—and give each student the role of historical docent for a small group of peers and adults. Students researched a few important sites along the trail, prepared activities, and drafted scripts to present on their day in the city as tour guides. (See Figure 3–26) History, science, and other content-heavy disciplines are great places to look for authentic writing opportunities.

Figure 3–26   Students Present as Tour Guides on the Freedom Trail

Belief: It Helps to Model a Path from Struggle to Optimism

When Elly was in my fifth-grade class, she was generally buoyant when it came time to write, even during revision. When I gave her a writing survey in June, she nearly tore a hole in the paper circling the most positive values on the Likert scale. It looked like a cyclone of revision fervor had touched down on the page. (See Figure 3–27.)

Sometimes I feel like Elly—my writing is flowing, ideas are flying off my fingertips onto the keyboard or page, the Muses are showering down inspiration. Other times, though, I feel like Miles. (See Figure 3–28.) I sigh over my "What the heck did I do?" moments as I look over my draft. The revision process can feel long, frustrating, or uncertain. I wonder, "Where am I going with this essay? What is this even about?!" Like in a moment of doubt during a high-wire act, I wonder, "How am I going to pull this off?" (I even felt this pessimism at times as I worked on this chapter about optimism!)

Figure 3–27   Elly's Survey Exudes Optimism

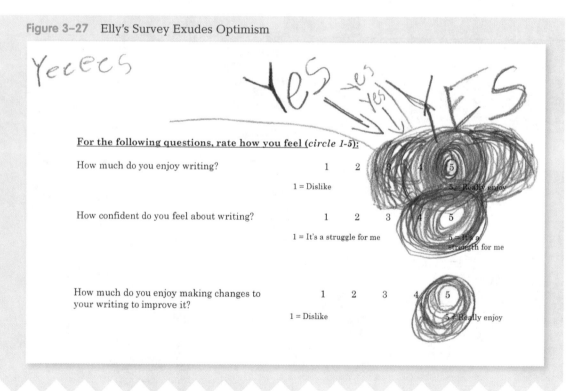

Figure 3-28   Miles' Survey Shows Mixed Feelings

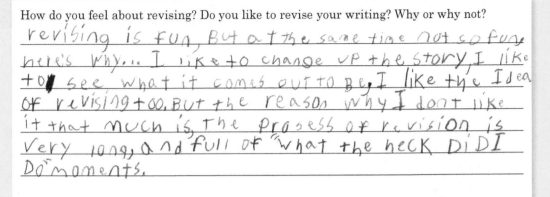

How do you feel about revising? Do you like to revise your writing? Why or why not?

revising is fun, But at the same time not so fun,
here's why... I like to change up the story, I like
to see, what it comes out to Be, I like the Idea
of revising too. But the reason why I dont like
it that much is, the prosess of revision is
Very long, and full of "what the heck DiDI
Do" moments.

As teachers, it helps to let our students know that it's natural to hit difficulties like this, but we can get through them. Sometimes writing just stalls
out, a draft falls short, or we're not sure what to do next. Rather than ignore
these problems, we can show students how to confront and move past them.
By helping them find a way through the challenges, we're helping them see
revision a bit more like Alja—"revising is like climbing a mountain, where
it's hard to get through it, but once you finish or get to the top you have a
beautiful view below you." We're showing them a path toward optimism.

Practice: Using Minilessons to Model Overcoming Difficulties

As teachers, we can share our thinking while we are facing revision snags
in our own writing—and explain how we overcome these challenges. Project
a draft of your own and read it aloud for students, pausing intermittently to
reflect on how you move forward, despite the struggles. Model how you use
the strategies in Figure 3–29.

Modeling How to Overcome Writing Difficulties

▶ *Navigate a writing rut.*

Model how to navigate a writing rut, like a moment of writer's block. Think aloud about how you got yourself unstuck. Show how to move forward by

trying a different prewriting approach, sketching your ideas visually (such as with storyboarding), rereading and hunting for hidden gems you've written, or skipping to a new, more energizing part of the writing.

"I'm writing this poem about a place from my childhood and I remembered hanging out under my porch in third grade. As you can see, I wrote for a bit, but I stalled out. I described the fun of being under there with some of my neighborhood buddies, hidden from view, but after about a paragraph, I didn't think I had more to say. Rereading this, though, I really like the lines 'Under the porch, I am a spy / Peering through the lattice.' To get unstuck, maybe I could try other lines like these—metaphors, like maybe 'Under the porch, I am a salamander' (since I had to wriggle my way through the damp dirt to get there) or '. . . I am a cave dweller' (since it was like a cave, and my tribe of friends would scratch out our plans in the dirt floor with sticks). I think I'll keep trying some new metaphors for who—or what—I was under that porch."

Figure 3–29   Modeling How to Overcome Writing Difficulties

▸ *Bounce back.*

You might show your students how you have bounced back and moved on from a dismal writing experience.

"I tried hard with this quickwrite for the last five minutes, but now as I read it, it's pretty 'meh.' I'm looking it over for some powerful lines, and it's like wading through a sea of sludge. But, hey, I know this happens sometimes as a writer—just like athletes sometimes have a tough workout that feels like a slog, where they're just getting through the exercises. I can shrug it off, let it go, and start tomorrow with a fresh idea."

▸ *Deal with tough feedback.*

Show your students how you process comments from readers that you might not agree with—how you accept some suggestions while letting others go.

"I'm writing my poem about playing horsey with my daughter when she was four, and some of my readers didn't realize that it was all a game of pretend. I was trying to make it seem like I was a real horse with lines like 'galloping in circles,' 'nudging you with my muzzle,' and 'speaking in soft whinnies and neighs,' but it sounds like this confused some people. I was surprised when some folks thought she was truly mad when I bucked her off. That was part of our game! At first I was a little defensive— like, 'How could they *not* get this?!'—but now I'm thinking I could try weaving in details so it's clearer. Like maybe I could use the word *daughter* somewhere instead of just *the cowgirl rider* and maybe I could show her laughing after I bucked her off. Some readers suggested I add other pretend games we played, but I'm going to let this comment go. I want my poem to focus in on just that one special memory."

(continues)

(continued)

(continued)

▸ *Sidestep perfectionism.*

Many of us are plagued with moments of doubt as writers; our "gremlin of self-criticism" tells us we will never measure up (Willems and Baty 2020). In striving for perfection, we end up with a blank page (or all our attempts scribbled into oblivion). Show your students how to silence their inner perfectionist by diving in, playing more, reflecting less, and staying immersed in the writing.

"Fiction writing is tough for me. I always feel like my story will never be as good as the ones I read. I get this little voice whispering negative thoughts in my ear, telling me my writing's no good. One writer I've read says to put our bully 'in a box' to shut him (or her) up (Lafferty 2017). I suppose you could get a real box, but mine's metaphorical. I'm going to lock my whispering bully up, and maybe I'll let him come up later, after I'm done writing.

"For now, I'm going to start my fiction piece using all the strategies I know to write fast and outrace my bully (in case he gets out of that box). I'll quickwrite, list, web, outline, maybe even sketch out some ideas. I'll start with a character, scene, or setting—whatever pops into my head. I hereby give myself permission to write cruddy plots, unrealistic dialogue, flat characters, and all the rest—but I'm filling these pages, dang it! Here goes."

A Final Thought on Optimism

As writers, most of us are too tough on ourselves. We constantly compare our writing with the published authors we revere—and feel acutely how we come up short. Forget criticism from others; we often bully *ourselves*. Chris Baty, founder of National Novel Writing Month, calls this "self-bullying" (2004, 42).

Optimism is the antidote. For this reason, it's one of the most important stances we can cultivate. Optimism reminds us to be kind and generous to ourselves, especially during the fragile, vulnerable moments of writing. It shifts our eyes and ears toward what's working with our drafts. It shows us how to dive in and feel the joy of discovery and just the fun of the process itself.

Optimism helps us pick up a pen in our uncertain fingers and trust that the words will come. It shines a light through difficulties and lets us hear an encouraging voice—our own. It's bullyproofing for writers.

4

Perspective-Taking

Writers Develop Through Awareness of and Connection with Audience

In early drafts, a poem is for me.

After that, it's for anyone, everyone.

—Mekeel McBride (Murray 1990, 39)

Sometimes you want to keep the skunk hidden for a while.

Andrew, one of my fifth graders, was writing a personal narrative about a camping trip in Maine with his family—a time when a late-night visitor ransacked their site. As he drafted in isolation, Andrew recounted each detail matter-of-factly: he brought out the curious, hungry skunk, front and center, into his piece—waddling, foraging, and rooting around their tent and all their belongings.

When it was time to revise, though, Andrew came to realize he had other choices. He might want to leave readers wondering what creature had caused such havoc, rather than give it away from the first paragraph. He realized he wanted less play-by-play and more whodunit mystery.

To keep his readers intrigued, Andrew added some tantalizing details and foreshadowing to his narrative: a rustling in the bushes; his dog barking; trash strewn everywhere; a glimpse of "a pink fuzzy nose" from an "unknown eavesdropper." He even decided to include a bit of misdirection, a red herring: at one point in the piece, he added, "'Maybe it's a coyote,' said Dad."

Andrew was becoming more aware of a potential audience at the other end of his lines. He began to anticipate his readers' reactions as they were reading, and it prompted him to make some meaningful changes to the way his story unfolded. According to Andrew, "In my first draft, I mentioned the 'black and white tail' too early. . . . I decided I wanted to give out clues more slowly, so readers would have to figure it out."

Using his imagination, and later through peer conferences, Andrew came to see his writing through a different set of eyes: his readers'. This is what we mean when we talk about perspective-taking with writing—gaining a second view on our work.

Wait a second. Rule one, according to most authors, is to write *for ourselves.* We need to hear our own voice first—explore our own ideas, figure out what resonates with *us*—rather than consider some imagined audience for our words. *Sound advice.*

It's true: we are our own first—and most important—readers, and yet it's important to keep our audience in mind, as well. "[With early drafts] I'm my audience and I don't know what I'm going to discover," Canadian novelist Margaret Laurence said. "But once the first draft is done, I do think of potential readers, in the sense that I feel that I want to make things as clear and effective as possible" (in Murray 1990, 38).

Would these lines be clear to someone else—and, if not, what else should be included? Would this sequence of events, description, or reasoning make sense to someone other than me? What emotions do I hope this part will evoke in readers? Would my readers be convinced by this argument? These are the questions we need to be asking ourselves as we're writing, in order to keep our readers engaged and informed, fed and happy. We need to be asking ourselves the question posted over the writer Catherine Drinker Bowen's desk: *"Will the reader turn the page?"* (Murray 1990, 36).

Figure 4–1 Justin and Carter Think About Their Readers

When writers have this awareness, they recognize the powerful effect their words can have on readers: they can delight or persuade, entertain or enlighten. They recognize the invisible thread that connects them, as writers, with their readers—that when they make a writing move, it prompts a reaction (from amused to bemused) in their audience. They recognize when they have left readers in the dark and need to add information to keep their meaning clear. These writers anticipate their audience's responses, and they listen carefully to actual comments they receive, so that they can adjust and revise based on these.

Take Tanmay, as he was drafting his book review to *Mr. Lemoncello's Library*. After a small-group conference, he realized his summary of the novel—perfectly clear to him—was still hazy for his listeners. He had included some intriguing details about the book but left his readers confused. *Why were the kids trapped in the library? How were they going to become millionaires? How did the contest work, and how was Mr. Lemoncello (whoever he was) involved in it?* As Tanmay listened to these and other questions—as he saw through his readers' eyes—he realized he needed to clarify several lines. "It helped me, the conference I did with students and teachers," Tanmay said, "because I got pen-striking questions."

Isn't that what we ultimately want, as writing teachers?! For our students to connect with their readers and listen, *really listen*, to their audience's reactions? To leave a conference with "pen-striking questions"—to be willing, even eager, to revise as a result? Absolutely—and we want them to begin to predict their audience's likely reactions as they are writing on their own. We want them to step into a reader's shoes and anticipate potential misunderstandings—places in the writing that need greater clarity, development, or focus.

So how do we foster this kind of perspective-taking? (See Figure 4–2.)

Belief: Writers Need to Anticipate Their Readers' Reactions

Many of our students don't have much experience with perspective-taking when they come to us. We see this when they plunge headlong into a story without enough context, leaving us, the readers or listeners, baffled. We think, "Wait, where were you? Who were you with? I can't tell if you're skateboarding or skiing—hold up!" In their excitement, they forget what we don't know as listeners, what background information we're missing.

It's likely they haven't been asked to think about their audience before. Perhaps the writing they were assigned didn't have much of an authentic audience to begin with.

Figure 4–2 Perspective-Taking

To foster perspective-taking in our student writers, we can, first off, just help them be aware that they *have* an audience, well before they get too far into a draft. "Who could be your audience for this piece?" Ask your students this and you may get shrugs or a vague notion ("Kids in my class, maybe?"), but posing the question can help a writer start to envision a potential reader and even their purpose for writing. When they wonder, "Who might be interested in reading this?" it can lead them to ask, "What's this piece mostly about? Why am I writing it?"

For John, writing about an in-the-park grand slam, there was only a fuzzy notion of an audience at first. Then he started to imagine possible readers— What about other baseball fans? How about those *without* much baseball knowledge? As he began thinking about audience, John realized he wanted to include the sights, sounds, and feelings he loved about the game. He decided to include those details (some) readers might relate to—but also to describe these in a way that even nonfans could understand. He revised to include the grip of the bat, the feeling of the cushion of the bag under his feet as he rounded the bases, the sensation of "feeling so alive right now."

To build perspective-taking, we need to ask students to anticipate the effect their words might have on their readers. Ask them about how different parts and lines will be received. Ask: "What does your audience need to know?" In this way, students can become more aware of what they might be missing in a draft—the information required for the events of the story to fit together, for the image in the poem to take shape in our minds, for the argument in the essay to leave us convinced. When we become aware of a possible reader, we begin to see that certain details—such as the pink nose of an eavesdropping spy—will kindle emotions and curiosity (or boredom or befuddlement).

Practice: Using Minilessons to Build Awareness of Our Audience

For John describing his grand slam and for all our writers, becoming conscious of their audience can spark some meaningful revisions. Ask your students to envision their potential readers—and anticipate those readers' reactions—through minilessons like the ones below.

Picture Your Reader

With this minilesson, ask your writers to envision a potential reader (an individual or a group). Whom do they picture? To whom would their writing appeal? Whom might their draft be addressing directly? As part of the process, ask: "What do you hope or imagine your reader will feel and think as they read your piece?"

In their civic action project, Eres and Alyssa wanted to take on climate change as an issue but weren't sure about an audience. However, as they researched about the burning of fossil fuels and the United States' culpability, they realized they wanted to write to the highest levels of our government. Their letter begins:

Dear President Donald J. Trump,

Climate change is very real. Many of our citizens don't believe in the subject, and we feel as though you would succeed in convincing many of them. The data is there, clear for all to see. Carbon emissions have

> skyrocketed over the past few years, and many are still blind to the subject.

Thinking of their audience, Eres and Alyssa knew they needed to address climate change denial, but they also wanted to enlist the president and appeal to the power of his position ("we feel as though you would succeed in convincing many of them"). Later in the letter, they also considered their reader's economic focus as they pointed out how clean energy (in the form of solar power) makes financial sense. They ended, again, with a nod to their specific audience:

> If America can lead the world in the fight against climate change like this, you will truly be making America Great Again.

Some writing projects, like a persuasive letter or essay, have a reader baked right in. For other pieces, thinking about our audience can be less clear. When Maryellen was writing poetry during the COVID-19 pandemic, it began as something just for her. As she revised, though, she realized her pieces were also speaking to other young adults like her around the world, with fears and uncertainties about the virus. This awareness helped shape her revisions.

> I'm stuck
>
> Stuck in a world where everything's the same
>
> Every day, stuck in a constant circle
>
> Every day I wonder
>
> When is it going to stop?
>
> Is it going to continue through the summer?
>
> Am I going to be stuck in this same room for 6 months?

According to Maryellen, she was writing for herself, but also "thinking of things [she] would say to someone in person." Her poem, she said, was a way to express her concerns (and eventually her hope), but it also energized her to imagine how other readers might connect and relate to her words. "I think my poem 'Stuck' really spoke to readers. I asked good questions and made a lot of people think."

Writer:

Title of Piece:

Picture Your Reader

Who is the **audience** for this piece of writing?

A. Sketch and label your potential reader:

My Readers:

B. What do you hope or imagine your reader will feel and think as they are reading your piece? In the margins around your drawing of your reader, add the feelings and thoughts you hope or imagine your audience will have while reading your piece.

Try these starters: I could picture . . .; I think . . .; I wonder . . .; This reminds me of . . .; I'm confused about . . .; When I read ___, I was feeling ___; The part ___ makes me ___; I'm interested in . . .; I love the part where . . .

Figure 4–3 Picture Your Reader Handout

For your minilesson, you might try a version of the Picture Your Reader handout. (See Figures 4–3 and 4–4.) Ask your writers to step into the shoes of their readers and see through those eyes. Try having them sketch, label, or describe a reader for their draft in progress. Ask students to jot callouts—little blurbs of thoughts or feelings—in the margins around their drawing of their imagined reader by answering some of the following:

- Who could be an audience for this piece?

- How might they react to different parts of my piece?

- Where would they have questions?

- What background info would this reader need for my ideas to make sense?

- What parts would resonate with them?

- Which lines would evoke strong emotions?

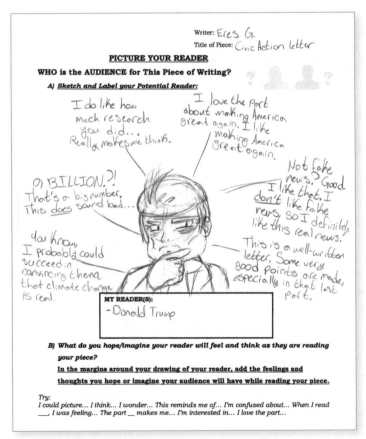

Figure 4–4   Eres' Picture Your Reader Example

Map Your Readers' Reactions

For this variation on the previous minilesson, put the students' writing piece itself at the center of the page. Then ask: "What do you imagine your reader might be feeling or thinking as they read certain lines or sections of your piece?"

Have students reread their draft, or a section of it, from the perspective of their audience. Ask them to pause occasionally to add margin notes—or digital comments in a Google Doc or MS Word file—showing their imagined reader's head or heart reactions to specific parts. Figure 4–5 is an example from Riley as she reviewed the first paragraph of her piece from a reader's perspective. As she predicted her audience's reactions, she realized she wanted to give them just enough information about this plunge into a river but also leave them intrigued.

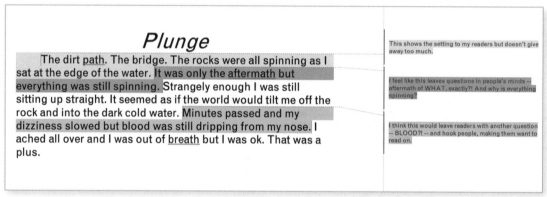

Plunge

The dirt path. The bridge. The rocks were all spinning as I sat at the edge of the water. It was only the aftermath but everything was still spinning. Strangely enough I was still sitting up straight. It seemed as if the world would tilt me off the rock and into the dark cold water. Minutes passed and my dizziness slowed but blood was still dripping from my nose. I ached all over and I was out of breath but I was ok. That was a plus.

This shows the setting to my readers but doesn't give away too much.

I feel like this leaves questions in people's minds -- aftermath of WHAT, exactly?! And why is everything spinning?

I think this would leave readers with another question -- BLOOD?! -- and hook people, making them want to read on.

Figure 4–5 Riley Mapped Her Readers' Reactions to Her First Paragraph

Write An Invitation to Readers

While your students are midrevision, you might try having them write a brief address—a one-paragraph introduction—directly to their imagined audience. *A caveat*: This is not intended to be an *explanation* of the writing piece—the type of description students often revert to when they kick off a writing share (e.g., "This is a story about the time I broke my finger."). This is an *invitation* to readers to share in the ideas and feelings of the writing. (See Figure 4–6.)

During the COVID-19 pandemic, I asked my students to keep a quarantine journal, a record of the strange and unprecedented times they were experiencing. As part of revising, I asked them to add an invitation to readers. "How could you introduce your quarantine journal to a reader one hundred years in the future? Or how might you introduce your journal to your future self (perhaps you in old age, looking back)?"

What an Invitation Might Include

▸ how the piece came to be

▸ whom it might appeal to—what kind of readers the writer would recommend it to

▸ what thoughts or feelings they had while writing it

▸ what thoughts or feelings they hope their audience will have as they read

▸ a reflection on their purpose—why they wrote it or what they hope for in writing it

Figure 4–6   What an Invitation Might Include

Here's an example from Sandro:

This was a time like no other in my life or anyone's in my generation. And that is why I am writing this, so that I can remember what happened when I get old and tell my story. This is a diary, a pandemic diary, or a journal or whatever you want to call it. I am writing about my experience with the coronavirus, what I see from my window, how I am dealing with it, and how others are, as well. It was a scary time for everyone and it really showed how we are all controlled by fear in some way. I feel like it puts humanity in its place.

For Cooper's introduction, he wrote to his future self. Thinking about his audience—even though it was himself—helped him identify a key theme, or message, he wanted to emphasize through his journal:

I put this journal together when I was 13 years old and living through the coronavirus (COVID-19). Hopefully, when you take a look at it, you can remember what happened back in the beginning of 2020. We can think back to those times and re-learn to love what we have today. Don't take things for granted. You will miss them. Trust me, at 13 years old we learned that lesson. Now, just remember it and enjoy the life we have while we can.

From,
Past Me

P.S. Please go out to restaurants a lot . . . I really miss them.

Whether you make invitations like these part of the revision process or an actual element in the final draft product, the goal is the same: to make our invisible readers materialize before our eyes.

Belief: Writers Need Connection over Diagnosis

Sometimes our conferences can feel like triage.

In *The Craft of Revision*, Don Murray (2001) discussed his countless writing conferences with students as extensive "trauma center experience" that informed his every move. Reading a first draft, he said, he sometimes felt like a "writing medic, deciding which section threaten[ed] the life of the essay and need[ed] immediate treatment" (85).

I've felt this urge, this rush to diagnose, though I know it's not what my young writers need most and it can be counterproductive. It's born out of a genuine desire to help them, to improve their writing, and it stems from my experience with similar writers (and writing pieces) in the past. But it can be a curse, this experience. Even though I know it's best not to begin a conference by jumping to suggestions, my experience—my inner triage medic—begins ticking off a mental list of fixes. I don't let these "immediate treatments" escape my lips, but do I betray them to my students unconsciously?

So I have had to remind myself: Giving feedback is not the same as having a meaningful conference. Learning happens in the context of relationships, and conferences are a way of building these relationships, not a means of feedback delivery. As Carl Anderson said, "Conferences are conversations," (2018, 4) and my goal is to connect with my student writers through these.

Practice: Conferring for Connection

One of the best ways to help my students is to highlight how their words affect me, moment by moment, as I'm reading them. Rather than identify the needs—and even strengths—of the writing piece, I can show them the power of their words. That each decision they make as writers elicits something in me, their reader.

My task . . . is, by the power of the written word,

to make you hear, to make you feel—

it is, before all, to make you see.

—Joseph Conrad (Murray 1990, 16)

Use the Movie of My Mind Technique

Try Peter Elbow and Pat Belanoff's (1995) Movie of My Mind tool, in which you tell writers what you are seeing, hearing, thinking, and feeling as you listen. As the writer reads aloud a piece, occasionally hit Pause and give your reactions in the form of "I" statements, to show how you are experiencing the piece (10). Periodically throughout the draft (it may be every paragraph—or more or less, depending on the piece), share the movie playing out in your mind in real time—which lines brought you joy, intrigue, or bewilderment.

When Autumn and I sat down for a conference, she started to hand over her short story and began to tell me about it—a thriller about a group of teenagers surviving a zombie apocalypse. Instead, I gently interjected and said, "Why don't you just read me what you have so far? I'll pause you occasionally to let you know what's going through my mind as a reader." She began reading:

> "Vines and leaves were slashed away with no mercy as the small group rushed their way through the seemingly never-ending forest. Even if they wanted mercy, there was no time for it, there weren't enough gas masks for everyone."

"Wow, Autumn!" I said. "I'm pulled right into this scene. I can almost see a group of people hacking through an overgrown jungle, trying to get through. I'm wondering who they are and where they are headed (I assume I'll learn more about this soon). When I hear the line about 'gas masks' though, I stop in my tracks. I'm wondering 'Why do they need gas masks in a forest? What kind of world is this?!' That line was unexpected, so I really want to find out more. . . ." Autumn cracked a slight smile and continued reading:

> "Leaves and moss clung to every tree, making no room for anything else. Purple flowers hung from the branches like acrobats from a trapeze, exhaling a pollen-like substance. Every chance that was given, the group swung at the flowers with dulled machetes."

"Let me hit Pause again," I interjected. "As a writer, you are zooming in on these purple flowers and their pollen as it is pluming up into the air. I'm thinking this might be important to the story." Autumn's face lit up. These plants, it will turn out, are the source of the zombie infection on Earth. As a writer, Autumn has set up an expectation in her readers—an itch—and my mental movie reflects it back to her.

In fact, the point of the Movie of My Mind approach is to show the writer the effect their lines have on the listener—how the moves they made set up a series of what Elbow calls "itches and scratches" (2012, 303). When Autumn included a flashback a few paragraphs later—a vivid description of the zombies themselves—I showed her how my expectations as a reader had been satisfied, how she had scratched the itch.

"Their skin had tints of green in some places, and it was peeling. . . . The skin was hanging there, over the decaying muscle. Sprouts were growing from inside the wounds, reaching out towards the air and sun. They curled in different directions, some with small purple buds on them, some with leaves sprouting. . . . They looked more plant than human, but you could tell. They were human. Or used to be human."

"Whoa! I'm riveted and grossed out—in a good way! When the zombies appeared, I wondered what had caused them to mutate, so when you included the detail about the purple buds, my brain went back to your lead. *Aha! It's the plants that are spreading it!*" As I was sharing my inner movie with Autumn, I was modeling the kind of conversation with her audience that I want her to internalize. Eventually, with some conferring and practice, this perspective-taking will become something a writer like Autumn just does naturally as she writes.

Alternatively, we can point out the moments when we become lost or our attention has waned—when the itch hasn't been scratched. Later in her story, one of Autumn's characters stumbles across a plant and it emits a cloud of pollen directly into her face. After she and the other protagonists escape, frantic but unharmed, I shared how my delight had turned to head-scratching. "I'm a little confused now, because I thought that Sophie would turn into a zombie based on what we read earlier." My mental movie let Autumn know there was breakdown—an inconsistency—in her story. This gave her a window into a reader's mind and a chance to consider how she might revise to make this section clearer.

The Movie of My Mind is such an effective conferring approach because it emphasizes the power writers have—the impact their words have on us. It changes the dynamic from one of compliance or compulsion—"Here's what you should do to change this piece"—to one of choices and decisions for the writer. It has the potential to lessen defensiveness for the writer, since we, the readers, aren't issuing demands, just honest responses.

Note: This conferring approach may be best to use once your students have a fairly developed draft—as well as some optimism and confidence about their writing in general—since they will hear not just their readers' kudos but their full range of reactions.

Have students confer with each other through Mind Reading

You certainly can, and should, teach your students to use the Movie of My Mind technique. Mind Reading involves a playful twist, making peer conferring into a kind of game. Students sit in pairs, one across from the other, a length of yarn or string between them to signify the imaginary thread between writers and readers.

Students take turns as writers, reading aloud their draft, or acting as listeners. Once the activity begins, listeners tune in, pausing the action when they react internally to a line or section of the text—when an emotion, an anticipation, a question, or a prediction bubbles up. When this happens, they give a gentle tug on the line. (If this is too distracting, students can tap on a desk or use another signal to pause the writer.)

The writer stops and tries to read the mind of their listener. "I think you (my reader) are feeling/thinking _____ right now because _____." Readers then reveal their real reactions, and the Mind Reading continues.

Note: As writers we certainly hope for certain responses in readers—a chuckle or a head nod at the right moment—but that's not always what we get. Readers may feel, think, or interpret our text in different ways than we predict, and that's to be expected (just as two readers will have different reactions and takeaways from the same book).

Keep in mind that you may want to put parameters on the game to keep it moving, such as encouraging writers to share short excerpts (as opposed to long pieces) or instructing listeners to tug just once per paragraph (or perhaps three to four times total during the piece).

Belief: Peer Conferences Are Tricky, But Worth It

Peer conferences can go awry in a hundred ways. Sometimes readers respond by harping on minor spelling issues when we want them to consider the big ideas in a piece. At times, listeners discharge heavy-handed criticism, leaving the writer to harden defensively—or wither under the feedback. Often, students' reactions can be like empty calories—sweet but without substance (the "Everything in your story was awesome!" variety). With these challenges, it can be tough for teachers to hand over control of conferences; some of us may have abandoned peer feedback or scaled it way back.

As a teacher, I often overlooked what a complex skill giving beneficial feedback is. I would put my students together and expect meaningful conferences to magically happen because, sometimes, they did. But when it happened, it was more luck than design. It takes time and support to develop these feedback skills, but teaching our students to do them well is worth the effort.

For one, peer conferences broaden the audience for our writers. As one student, Lauren, said to me, "I like conferencing with peers more than adults, because my main audience is going to be kids anyway, so knowing what they think is more helpful (not that I don't enjoy receiving your feedback!)." As we've talked about, predicting our imagined audience's reactions is an important skill, but so is closely observing how an *actual* audience responds to our writing. Lauren said, "[Seeing and] understanding how [my writing] is going to make other people react is different than just reading it myself, and deciding that is what everyone is going to think."

We can make our peer conferences more effective by

- explicitly teaching students the speaking and listening skills involved (rather than assuming they've mastered them);

- gradually releasing responsibility for conferring (rather than sending kids off on their own prematurely and then being frustrated when things get messy); and

- using a range of sharing structures (progressing from more safe and simple to more involved and sophisticated).

Practice: Using Minilessons to Teach Conferring Skills and Foster Connection

I no longer expect my writers and readers to come in with the skills they need to give (and receive) effective feedback. I teach these explicitly when I'm introducing my writing workshop norms at the beginning of the year.

I start by asking the class, "What does helpful feedback look like and sound like?" and developing common understandings my students can refer back to, time and time again. Figure 4–7 lists some of the comments my classes typically come up with.

Teaching readers to give feedback like this reaps lasting rewards. When students read each other's work closely—when they take care to give these kinds of comments—it builds trust and forges deep connections. Yes, it will give your writers a greater awareness of audience, but it will also deepen the relationships in your room. We all want to foster a sense of community among our students; reader responses like the ones in Figure 4–7 make it happen.

Feedback is a two-way street, and the writer—no surprise—plays a key role as well. In a separate minilesson with your class, brainstorm the writer's responsibilities before, during, and after a conference. Figure 4–8 lists some of the concepts that usually spring up in minilessons with my students.

Practice: Sharing Using a Gradual Release of Responsibility

I used to kick off peer conferences without the preparation described here, and then I'd grumble to myself when some groups floundered. No one is born an expert at giving feedback—students *or* teachers. So, in addition to minilessons, I also build students' expertise by rolling out conferences more slowly and systematically.

I start with whole-group feedback—teachers and peers together—so I can model the behaviors and comments described in the last section. When my class seems ready, we move on to small-group feedback, with me handpicking groups and rotating table to table. We preview our responsibilities as readers and writers ("Remember what helpful feedback looks and sounds like? Let's take a quick look before we break out into groups."). Sometimes we debrief as a class after peer conferences ("How did we do with giving and receiving feedback? What did we do well? What could we work on for next time?").

What Does Helpful Feedback Look and Sound Like?

What does helpful feedback *look* like?

▶ Listeners face the writer (in pairs, in small groups, or as a whole class).

▶ Our bodies and facial expressions show interest and respect (we are sitting up, focused and attentive to the writing, not having side conversations).

▶ Readers give our reactions out loud and in writing (we might take turns sharing reactions when the author finishes or jot down our thoughts so the writer can refer back to them).

What does helpful feedback *sound* like?

▶ Listeners use "I" statements. ("I smiled and chuckled to myself when you described how your dog is a great cuddler and also how she snores.")

▶ Listeners share our head and heart reactions as we listen. ("When you wrote . . . , I was feeling or thinking . . .")

▶ Listeners provide specific comments. ("This line stood out to me because . . ."; "The talking in your story sounded like the way real brothers and sisters fight"; "I didn't understand the end—I couldn't tell if you fell after the ski jump or landed it. . . .")

▶ Listeners give kind *and* honest responses. Feedback usually includes a mix of the strengths of the piece and some constructive suggestions, starting with the positives. But writers can tell when their audience isn't being forthright—when they lavish vague praise on a shaky piece—so it's important that readers give genuine, though always respectful, reactions.

▶ Listeners share questions we had while listening—questions about parts that were unclear to us or that we were genuinely curious about. ("Who was with you when your dog got hit by the car? What did they say or do?")

▶ Listeners provide suggestions and what-ifs. When we offer advice, it's a suggestion for the writer to think about, not a directive to follow. These could be in the form of "What if . . . ?" ("What if you told us more about what your cat would do if he were an astronaut in outer space?") or "You might want to . . ." ("You might want to try adding more about what you love about football.").

Figure 4–7   What Does Helpful Feedback Look and Sound Like?

The Writer's Responsibilities for Conferences

With your students, brainstorm a writer's responsibilities before, during, and after a conference.

Before

▶ Consider which piece of writing I want to share. *Which piece am I most excited about and ready for other students to hear? Which piece could I use some help with?*

▶ Consider what parts of my piece I might want help with. *What part or aspect of my writing could be improved? What am I stuck on or unsure about?*

During

▶ Read smoothly and clearly (with enough volume and clarity for listeners).

▶ Listen with an open mind when readers give their reactions, questions, and suggestions.

▶ Ask a follow-up question if I don't understand something my audience has said or written.

After

▶ Carefully consider my readers' responses. *Which comments stay with me? Which might be helpful to me as I revise?*

▶ Think about the strengths my readers noticed. *How could I use these strengths in other places (in this piece or other writing)?*

▶ Consider making some substantial changes, based on some of the feedback from my audience. *What questions or suggestions would help develop my writing? How could I add, change, or remove parts to make my writing clearer and stronger, based on my readers' comments?*

Figure 4–8   The Writer's Responsibilities for Conferences

As the year progresses, I give students more autonomy and independence for their conferences—more choice in their feedback groups or partners and the types of feedback they want.

Practice: Mixing Up Peer Conferring to Keep Things Fresh

Keep peer conferences interesting by using a range of formats and approaches. (See Figure 4–9.)

Ways to Vary Peer Conferring

Consider the following aspects of peer conferring:

▸ *Group size and structure:* My first year teaching, there was one way we shared writing: a single author at the rocking chair, reading to the entire group. It took *forever* for everyone to have a turn. The routine got stale. Now, I might begin with whole-class shares, then move to small groups, and finally transition to partners, but it's not a linear progression. It's most effective (and fun) when we mix it up. (See Figures 4–10 through 4–12.)

▸ *Types of feedback:* Feedback can range from positives only, to adding questions, suggestions, and what-ifs. Some examples:

  ▪ A "more, please" response, where listeners share what they wanted to hear more about in a piece. This approach is best when writers are still developing ideas or finding the focus of their piece.

  ▪ A say-it-back response, where readers summarize, or say back, what the piece seemed to be mainly about. This is most useful when drafting, so writers know if what they think their main focus is matches what readers think (Elbow and Belanoff 1995, 9).

  ▪ A target response, where the writer asks for help with something specific that seems off about their draft. This one is harder for many students (who are often unsure what to ask for). Try suggesting they identify something concrete at first, something they can point to directly in the text (such as the title, lead, ending, or a certain passage). For example, Hannah, who was generally quite shy, reached out to ask her classmates for suggestions on her title. "I was out of ideas, and I didn't really like 'Toothless,'" she said of her draft (about a sisterly scuffle that ended in a trip to the dentist). "I knew

Figure 4–9   Ways to Vary Peer Conferring

(continues)

(continued)

the class could help me come up with lots more ideas." Targeted feedback worked for Hannah because it was later in the school year, when her classmates had grown in their feedback skills and she had come to trust them more as readers.

▸ Several of these ideas—and other great feedback strategies—can be found in Peter Elbow and Pat Belanoff's wonderful guide *Sharing and Responding* (1995).

▸ *Modes of sharing both writing and feedback:*

- aloud (for writers, their draft; for readers, their comments)
- silently, on paper or digitally

Figure 4–10   Small-Group Conferring

Figure 4–11   One-on-One Conferring

Figure 4–12   Whole-Class Conferring

Belief: Writers Need a Reader They Can See (More Than a Virtual One)

Our brains are wired to learn socially, interpersonally. Patricia Kuhl (2010), a researcher from the University of Washington, gave infants Chinese lessons; one group got face-to-face tutoring while the other received the identical material via video. Both groups of babies were engrossed during the sessions, but it was those who were taught in person who grasped the Chinese sounds at an astounding rate. Their "social brain" (Kuhl's term) was activated through direct eye contact and other interactions with their tutors. The children on screens? They paid rapt attention but showed "no learning whatsoever" (Kuhl 2010).

Teaching in the age of COVID-19, was there any doubt that something was missing during remote learning? Technology is a remarkable tool that helped us salvage a semblance of school during the quarantine of 2020, but did anyone believe that our connection with students was as authentic or meaningful through a screen?

And yet, if you're anything like me and the colleagues I know, your writing comments—and those of your students—have become increasingly digital. Why are we gravitating more to Google Docs for feedback? It's more efficient; we are continually pressed for time, and online comments allow us to get to more drafts. It makes management a breeze; most students happily plug right into laptops and chug away. Maybe it feels safer or less chaotic. Perhaps it's the fact that all our feedback is *right there*—encapsulated in the margins of MS Word, not left behind or lost in a folder. I once visited a classroom to observe "peer conferences"; for thirty minutes, I watched as students' eyes were fixed on their computers, like isolated islands, clicking out comments on classmates' drafts with hardly a word spoken.

There was something profoundly sad about this, and here's the rub: it doesn't really work, at least not any better. As I've watched my students receive more and more digital feedback—as I've taken part in it and led the charge—I haven't noticed any real improvement in their willingness to revise. They are riveted to their screens and, yes, they make some changes, but just as often they (seemingly) ignore the comments in the margins or look overwhelmed by them.

Something is lost in translation when we give only virtual feedback, physically distancing writer from reader. Writers can't see their audience's bursts of laughter, the looks of surprise and delight, the spontaneous leaning in—or the glassy-eyed stares when their interest flags. The efficiency of digital comments is an illusion if it doesn't really help our writers revise.

This isn't a call to arms to shun our laptops and Google Docs. You and I will continue to use the comment feature in Word, but let's not do it exclusively. Digital feedback needs to be coupled with face-to-face interaction. Whenever we can, let's prioritize the interpersonal.

Practice: Conferring with Peers, Live and In Person

Maybe, like me, you've noticed your writing workshop shifting increasingly to online feedback—and felt uneasy about the digital divide it creates between writers and readers. If so, this is a reminder, a call to recommit to peer conferences, out loud and in person.

A disclaimer *and* a warning: The conferring structure here (see Figure 4–14) won't be earth-shattering, *but* it may rock your status quo. It's a basic protocol with endless variations—one that keeps me honest when I feel too much drift to the digital and want to foster more perspective-taking.

Figure 4–13   Izzy and Connor Sit Side by Side to Confer

Peer Conferring. Live and in Person

1. *Writers and readers sit facing each other* in a small group. (Pairs can sit across from each other, but I encourage sitting side by side, so partners can look at a draft together; see Figure 4–13.)

2. *Writers read their draft aloud.* If possible, try to have writers read their piece twice—the first time for readers to take in the words, the second to have time to make comments. Some students may balk at reading their writing aloud, especially in older grades. It can feel vulnerable and awkward, but it's incredibly important to hear the sound of our own words (more on this risk in Chapter 7). Having hard copies for readers is great as well (since we process best by hearing *and* seeing).

3. *Readers hold their thinking by taking notes.* After the initial reading, the process pauses so readers can jot down impressions. Then writers read their draft again, during which readers add to their notes. The second time through gives the audience a chance for more thoughtful comments since their ears (and eyes) are already primed to the piece. (See Figures 4–15 and 4–16 for two worksheets I have students use at times. One is more traditional, asking for strengths, questions, and suggestions, and the other is a written extension of the Movie of My Mind approach, asking for head and heart reactions while reading.)

4. *Readers (briefly) share out their responses and comments,* starting with the strengths of the piece (or their positive reactions).

5. *Writers listen carefully to the audience's feedback.* The goal is to soak up the audience's comments and resist the urge to be defensive or to answer every question given. (I often suggest, "We'd love you to answer that burning question, but in your draft.")

6. *Readers hand their written feedback to writers.*

Figure 4–14   Peer Conferring, Live and in Person

Writing Conference Form

Writer's Name:————————————————————————————

Title of Writing Piece:——————————————————————————

Response from:——————————————————————————
(Listener's/Reader's Name)

Date:——————————

Strengths

(For example, "I noticed . . ."; "The part that sticks with me is . . ."; "You did a strong job trying . . .")

Questions

(For example, "I wondered . . . "; "Could you explain more about . . . ?")

Suggestions and What-ifs

(For example, "What if you . . . ?"; "One thing you could try is . . .")

Figure 4–15   Peer Conference Form—Strengths, Questions, Suggestions

Writing Conference Form
The Movie of My Mind

Writer's Name:_____

Title of Writing Piece:_____

Response from:_____

Date:_____ *(Listener's/Reader's Name)*

- Ask the writer to pause during their draft when you have a head or heart reaction.
- Take notes on the place in the draft where you reacted, then describe the movie of your mind (what was happening inside your mind as you read or listened).
- Share your reactions with the writer at the end.

When you wrote . . .	I was thinking/feeling/wondering . . .
When you wrote . . .	I was thinking/feeling/wondering . . .
When you wrote . . .	I was thinking/feeling/wondering . . .

Figure 4–16   Peer Conference Form—the Movie of My Mind

See? Nothing mind-blowing, *but* I'll bet many of us have skimped on conferences like these, or we've assumed that digital peer feedback would fit the bill. Perhaps we felt we didn't have the time—because, no doubt about it, conferring in person does take more of it.

As for me, I'm not turning my back on all online feedback, but I know learning happens best in person, in a social context. To have a true writer-reader think tank—and spark real revision—we need the thinkers face-to-face, not laptop-to-laptop.

Practice: Revising with Postconference Reflections

OK, our writers get all kinds of peer feedback, but then what? I often use a sheet like the one in Figure 4–17 after peer conferences to prompt my students to take action. I remind them: "You won't agree with every suggestion. Some questions might take you in a different direction than you want to go with your piece. You don't need to—and shouldn't try to—address every single comment from readers. Still, some feedback should ring true to you and inspire some changes in your writing.

"Think about the comments that resonate with you. Decide on a few specific actions you can take to revise, based on the feedback you were given."

Figure 4–17   Koushik's Postconference Reflection

Writer's Name: _____Koushik_____   Date: __10/8_____

Title of Writing Piece: _____Snapshot writing piece._____

POST-CONFERENCE REFLECTION

Think about the feedback you received on your draft from readers. Read over their comments. Review the questions and suggestions they gave you.

List 3 or more actions you might take to revise your piece, based on the feedback you were given.

[*For example:* questions readers had that you might clarify in your draft; parts you might expand on that they were curious about; changes you might make based on their suggestions/reactions; etc.]

Based on the commentes I received, I decided to add some more sensory details, and also add some emotions, like happy, or cheerful, and add what the course looks like. I also am going to add some more interior monologe, and a description on how nervous I was. I also need to come up with a good title.

After Koushik shared his draft about a robotics competition, he realized some important pieces were missing. As he listened to readers, it became clear: they couldn't hear his thoughts—the worries swirling in his brain before the big event—or feel his pride at the end when his team took gold. His classmates, many of whom were unfamiliar with robotics, also couldn't picture the setting (*Was the robot showdown in a packed gymnasium or a quiet classroom?*). "Based on the comments I received, I decided to . . . add some [of my] emotions . . . and add what the course looks like," Koushik wrote. "I also am going to add some more interior monologue, and a description [of] how nervous I was."

Figure 4–18 Students Confer and Then Reflect Post Conference

When John read his draft aloud to his small group, their comments made him aware that his readers were still foggy about some key parts of his piece (the baseball story with the inside-the-park home run mentioned earlier). Following his peer conference, John jotted down a few actions to take, including "Face the camera [toward] the crowd." His readers told him they wanted to know how the onlookers in the stands reacted when the main character unexpectedly smacked the grand slam, so John decided to turn his attention—his writer's camera—to the crowd. His readers also helped him recognize he needed to show where "the ball goes"; they couldn't see the ball's trajectory yet—what happened after the initial crack of the bat (*Was it hit deep to the outfield? Did the other players chase after it? Where was the ball when the batter was running the bases?*). The answers to these questions were in John's mind, but—after listening to readers—he suddenly realized they weren't on the page. Yet. (See Figure 4–19.)

Connecting with our readers—becoming aware of what they're thinking and predicting how they might react—helps us know whether to show the baseball, turn the teenager into a zombie, or keep the skunk out of sight.

Figure 4–19   John's Postconference Reflection

Writer's Name: __John__   Date: _____
Title of Writing Piece: __4 fkh homer__

POST-CONFERENCE REFLECTION

Think about the feedback you received on your draft from readers. Read over their comments. Review the questions and suggestions they gave you.

List 3 or more actions you might take to revise your piece, based on the feedback you were given.

[*For example:* questions readers had that you might clarify in your draft; parts you might expand on that they were curious about; changes you might make based on their suggestions/reactions; etc.]

- Face The camra TWO The crowd
- The weahter
- Were The ball goes

5

Flexible Thinking

Writers Develop by Staying Open to New Ideas and Approaches

What prompts students to revise with gusto? What makes our writers adopt the stances of a writer's mindset? Often, it's a bit of a mystery. For Henry, it turned out to be an unusual sketch, a love of Tolkien, and a serious sweet tooth.

"I'm obsessed with peppermint bark—you know, the homemade holiday cookie?—and one day I was thinking about a praying mantis (no, I don't know why!). Anyway, the two started to mix together in my head—peppermint, praying mantis, peppermant . . . Peppermantis! So, I took a piece of paper and I drew a praying mantis with arms and legs made of candy canes, a body of white chocolate, a plating of dark chocolate, and peppermint chunks on top." Not long after, Henry was sitting in my language arts class, stumped about what to write. According to Henry, he had "hit a mental roadblock"—until he suddenly remembered his Peppermantis sketch. "It was like when a pirate came upon an unguarded merchant ship, or when a Viking found a nice monastery full of monks and gold stuff. It came to me: the vision of a land made of candy, a fight between good and bad!" (See Figure 5–1.)

For students like Henry, flexible thinking means being open to inspiration, wherever it comes from. Henry started strong, taking his Peppermantis sketch and crafting a promising draft—one with a vivid villain who "terrorized the gingerbread men and women of Caramelway village . . . the sharp tips of its candy-cane legs leaving deep tracks in the powdered sugar." It was a wonderful beginning—but only one paragraph long. At first, it looked like the piece would remain that way, unchanged, relatively undeveloped.

But Henry continued to reflect on his hopes for the story, to experiment with new possibilities, and to mull over some of the conversations from our conferences. He began adding characters, such as the original—"O.G."— Gingerbread Man. He imagined—and then zoomed in on—several specific scenes (including one where the Peppermantis lays waste to the town, "like Smaug the dragon").

Henry thought about his goals for his piece, and the tone he wanted it to have. "I had started off thinking it would be a classic, old-timey fairy tale, but over time, I realized I wanted to play off that and make it into a cheesy parody—in a good way! I thought, 'I don't want this. . . . I want that.' I added some cringey humor in places." As he revised, Henry's humor and voice began emerging—like in his lines describing the Gingerbread Man "taking up arms, and then reattaching them with icing." Or the moments when the hero readied for battle: "He ran and ran as fast as he could, passing through many towns, gathering his weapons. By which I mean he found a gumdrop, put it on a stick and said, 'Good enough.'"

Henry decided he wanted to include a plot twist—the villain as a victim. "The Peppermantis started as an evil monster, but I wanted it to be a little different. Like maybe he was misunderstood."

Henry kept playing with, in his words, "new routes" for his story.

Figure 5–1 Henry's Peppermantis Sketch

As he did, his piece kept improving—both the quality of his draft and his enthusiasm for it. He was willing to hold off on saying, "I'm done," and allow himself to stay *in process*.

This is what it means to think flexibly. As writers, we often experiment with fresh ideas before putting the finishing touches on a draft. When we're thinking flexibly, we try to consider what our piece needs, rather than rush to complete it. To stay open to new approaches and even criticism (within limits). To have the confidence to try something novel and creative with our writing but also the humility to know that great ideas might come from listening to others. To have the curiosity to seek out fresh solutions to make our writing the best it can be.

So how can we foster this openness in our writing classrooms? (See Figure 5–2.)

Whoa! As I reread this quickwrite, it surprises me—I didn't know I thought this! Maybe I could explore it more . . .

How could I look at this topic differently—maybe zoom in on one part? Or try to see the "big picture" and figure out what I want to say?

What could I try with this piece—what does it need? A new ending? A different point of view?

Where could I go with this piece? I'll play with some "What if?" and "I wonder?" questions and see where they take me . . .

Figure 5–2   Thinking Flexibly

Belief: Writing Should Involve Discovery, Play, and New Ways of Seeing

When I write poems I try to get at the mystery of my subject. . . .
I mean the truth about the subject that isn't obvious,
that's under the surface.
—Ralph Fletcher (Janeczko 2002, 22)

For me the initial delight is in the surprise of remembering
something I didn't know I knew.
—Robert Frost (Murray 1990, 101)

Writing and rewriting are a constant search for
what it is one is saying.
—John Updike (Murray 1990, 114)

Meaning is not what you start out with but what you
end up with.
—Peter Elbow (1973, 15)

One of the purposes—and joys—of writing is discovering what we think *through the writing process*, not knowing what we're going to say ahead of time. Start reading authors' reflections on their own process, and this sentiment is so commonplace it almost goes without saying. Except, *how many of our students know this? How many of us approach writing this way?*

My oldest daughter, a rising senior, was recently brainstorming ideas for her college essay. She was just getting started listing possible essay topics when her stress rose up and she began chopping off potential ideas at the knees. "OK, but what the heck am I going to *say* about Merrowvista [her longtime summer camp] or about learning to love dance so late in high school?" Emma's uncertainty—and mounting frustration—was that she didn't know if her topics would bear any fruit, if they would lead to any big ideas or insights (the kind

she had read in model college essays). She felt—as most of us do—that she should know what she was going to say *before* she began. But these insights often come *as we're writing* (or after)—as a product of our writing, not as a precursor to it. (*Note*: This is not something a stressed-out high school student wants to hear when her first-draft essay is nearly due.)

What I want my students (and daughter) to know is that writing can be like plunging under water, like jumping in from the edge of a lake. We can see a bit of what's under the surface before we leap—before we begin writing—but just the outer shape of things (the hazy outlines of rocks, sand, and maybe some leafy muck). Once we immerse ourselves—into the water and the writing—what's beneath the surface is often different than we expect. We might feel around with our fingers or open our eyes briefly and notice the topography of the lake bottom—the colors and textures of boulders, the unexpected nooks to swim to and explore. Reviewing our writing and searching for surprises is like submerging again in the same spot, this time with goggles or a mask. We notice layers of shimmering fish crisscrossing around our legs where we thought it was lifeless. A little cavern where we thought it was flat. The beautiful striations in a seemingly drab stone.

When we see writing as a way to discover meaning—to find out what we think, to dive down under the surface of topics and get at their mystery—we're naturally more flexible with our approach to it. We're more inclined to pause, turn our heads, and investigate different directions before racing to the end. When students have time and encouragement to experiment, play, and explore ideas—to open their eyes under water—they are often surprised by what they discover (both the ideas they come up with and the direction their writing takes).

Practice: Prewriting by Searching for Surprises

After quickwriting, listing, webbing, or whatever prewriting you ask students to try, have them pause and review what they've written. As students reread their words, ask them to circle a surprise. (See Figure 5–3.)

One of my students, Joey, had done some quickwriting about how much he loved swimming on our local team, the Otters. Most of his quickwrite was about

Circle a Surprise

A surprise could be an unexpected

▶ tension,

▶ question,

▶ thought or feeling, or

▶ idea that itches—that you want to explore further.

Figure 5–3   Circle a Surprise

the joys of the sport, but he was drawn to one line that surprised him because it alluded to the struggles: "I know how to lose and don't show pain because I know the only one I'm racing is myself." Joey starred this line, and, several months later, it became the seed for his narrative "Under a Minute," about pushing aside the pain and disappointment and striving to beat his longstanding goal in the hundred-yard freestyle. (See Figure 5–4.)

Figure 5–4 Joey's Example of Circling a Surprise

When something unexpected emerges, it's important to pay attention to it. Figure 5–5 includes some things to consider as you help your students search for surprises.

Practice: Drafting by Changing One Significant Thing

Keeping a sense of discovery and openness can be harder the further into a draft we get. Sentences that were once malleable begin to calcify the more we work on a piece, which is natural. Encourage flexible thinking by asking students to experiment early in the writing process—before their drafts start to harden—and add an element of play.

Searching for Surprises

▶ Make it a regular habit. Have students circle a surprise either immediately after prewriting, the following day, or even weeks (or months) later. Tell them that taking time to review our words—and mine them for the unexpected—is something writers do.

▶ Model this self-discovery with your own writing. Show them a prewrite of your own and try a think-aloud, showing your openness to surprise and new directions. Hunt for what Don Murray calls "the instigating line" and share your running reflections about it (2001, 5). For example: "I started this quickwrite thinking about my memories of my grandmother, and what stands out is this line about the smells in her kitchen. I'd forgotten about all the delicious smells! I think I might focus on that one idea and just write about the wonderful aromas as she was cooking. Maybe it will be a poem or a little snapshot in time."

▶ Remind students that their minirevelations can be places to pivot in their writing. They might find one small part to explore (as in the example about my grandmother's kitchen), shift to a different focus, recall an anecdote or detail that illustrates a point perfectly, or discover a whole new piece to try.

▶ Take time to have students share their surprises with each other, even briefly.

Figure 5–5   Searching for Surprises

Together with your students, brainstorm and post ways to mix it up with a draft. See Figure 5–6 for some ideas of ways to change one significant thing in a draft.

Perhaps try making this into a game. You might play with revision possibilities by trying one of the activities in Figure 5–7. While this might seem like a cutesy gimmick, it's something real artists do. Musician Brian Eno created the Oblique Strategies deck of cards with artist Peter Schmidt to help offer possibilities to overcome creative block.

Changing One Significant Thing in a Draft

▸ **point of view** (e.g., switch to a different narrator; take a piece in first person and switch it to third)

▸ **the lead or ending**

▸ **verb tense** (e.g., shift from past to present tense)

▸ **voice, tone, or mood** (e.g., try to evoke a different emotion, like injecting humor in a previously serious piece)

▸ **time or structure** (e.g., mix up chronological order; change an informational piece's cause-and-effect structure to a problem-and-solution one)

▸ **length** (e.g., cut out as many lines as you can)

▸ **sentence or paragraph length or variety** (e.g., add a paragraph that's one sentence long; add short sentences—ones that are five words or less in length)

▸ **genre** (e.g., take a memoir and turn it into a news story or a haiku)

Figure 5–6 Changing One Significant Thing in a Draft

Practice: Revising by Adjusting the Camera

Writing is not writing skills, but knowing how to see. . . .
There are people who can't read or write who are novelists.
They've got two lenses. A telephoto lens for big pictures
and a lens a dentist would use.

—Carolyn Chute (Lane 2016, 33)

Helping our students to think flexibly about their writing means giving them different lenses through which to see. With metacognition, we showed them how to look *egocentrically*—to explore their personal reflections and decisions

Playing with Possibilities

▶ *Rolling revisions:* **Choose six (or even twelve) options from your brainstormed class list of ways to change a text and have students each roll a die (or dice). Assign a number to each possible different change, and have them commit to trying whichever one they roll (for example, 1 = different point of view; 2 = different lead or ending).**

▶ *Spin the revision wheel:* **Take a couple of pieces of oaktag or poster board and a brass brad (those little metal winged fasteners for paper) and—ta-da!—you have the makings for a revision wheel. Around the borders of the spinner, write the different options for revision experimentation that you brainstormed. When your wheel is complete, have students each take a spin. The game: to try whatever they land on (change genre; cut length; etc.) with their draft.**

Whatever approach you choose—and whatever change your students roll or land on—ask them to give it an honest try. Take time to play, and ask them mix up an emerging draft.

Figure 5–7   Playing with Possibilities

about a draft. In the chapter on perspective-taking, we worked on developing a reader's view, helping students to see in an *allocentric* way.

We can have students try two additional lenses: (1) a *macrocentric* view, in which we think about the big picture (the overall purpose, themes, or ideas we're striving for), and (2) a *microcentric* view, in which we zoom in on particular sections to see how they enhance (or stray from) those big ideas.

When you ask your students to step back with a wide-angle lens, it prompts them to consider what their piece is truly about. When Kalen wrote about her grandfather's death, the topic was incredibly important to her, but she couldn't find her focus as she drafted. Should she write about special times with him? Was her story about the moment she heard the devastating news? Stopping to think, "What's this really about?" helped her find the core of her piece: her feelings of guilt that she showed little emotion when her grandfather first passed. Pausing to think about the big picture helped Kalen find the heart of her piece:

> I didn't believe it happened, so I ignored it. Pushed it to the back of my head. That was my way of coping with the way I felt. I couldn't deal with any more pressure than I had. It was too hard. Now that I look back on it, I kind of feel horrible, even heartless. Why didn't it just hit me then, right when it happened?

You can also have your students adjust their writer's camera by choosing important moments to zoom in on. As they direct their energy to a small section of their writing—like using a dentist's lens—they can reveal significant details and use their senses, thoughts, or feelings.

When Nick described a hike up a mountain in Acadia National Park, he took a microcentric view by describing his feelings at each rung of a ladder he had to climb. As he began, he wrote, "I feel my soul leave my body as I step onto the first rung. . . . It's too late to turn back now though." Later, he reached the second rung. "I don't know what to do, so I just stand there for a little bit and think to myself, *This is probably the most dangerous mountain I will ever hike, and I'm only eight.*" He started to cry as he reached the third rung and looked down—"Instant regret"—to see "[he was] not just on a hill, [he was] on top of a straight drop to death."

Try having your students zoom in—on a moment in time, on an important object, or on a part of the setting. Or have them pan out to view the entirety of their draft. Use the charts in Figures 5–8 and 5–9—or modify them—to help your students adjust their mental cameras and develop different ways of seeing.

Belief: Teachers Need to Talk Up Flexibility and Pause to Stretch

When I asked Sarah, a fifth grader, if she liked revising, she said, "Sometimes . . . [when] my writing transforms into something I didn't expect." For Andrew, revision is enjoyable when "it opens up new possibilities with a piece." These rewards of revision and thinking flexibly aren't always apparent to our students, though, so we need to talk them up. We should point out how it feels when we have a flash of fresh insight through our writing, when we discover something we "didn't know we knew." The sense of fun when we

Looking at the Big Picture

Take a WIDE-ANGLE view.
Adjust your writer's camera to see the big picture of your piece.
What is your piece really about? What's the heart of it?

Answer this in one paragraph:

Now, answer in just one sentence:

Lastly, give your answer in one to three words:

Figure 5–8 Looking at the Big Picture

Focusing on a Detail

> **ZOOM IN.**
> Adjust your writer's camera by zooming in on the details
> of an important scene, part, or topic in your draft.

List two to three important scenes, parts, or topics from your draft:

A. _____

_____

B. _____

_____

C. _____

_____

Next, choose one part to zoom in on. Circle or highlight it above.

Now, dive in! Zoom in on this scene, part, or topic and picture it in detail.
Describe it while keeping the following pointers in mind:

▸ Use your senses. What could you see? Hear? Feel? Smell? Taste?

▸ Focus on a powerful image. Describe what you see in detail. Be specific.

▸ Use your thoughts or feelings. What was running through your mind then—
or what do you think or feel about this now?

_____

_____

_____

_____

_____

Figure 5–9   Focusing on a Detail

experiment with our words and something exciting emerges. The pride we feel when we see the depth and scope of improvements we've made to a writing piece—where we started versus where we ended up. We can highlight these feelings when we periodically hit the Pause button during writing workshop and ask students to try something different.

As we're talking up flexibility, it's important to remember that our words, as teachers, can encourage—or undercut—this sense of openness. We need to use language that promotes flexible thinking—and to monitor ourselves when we slip into fixed-mindset language. The words we use as we talk about writing and revision matter; they can support more intrinsic motivation (showing the inherent value and even pleasure of revising) or reinforce more extrinsic motivation (e.g., revising for a grade or only in response to teacher demands).

Practice: Shifting the Language We Use in Writing Workshop

Take an honest look at your own speech patterns and make some conscious shifts toward language that fosters flexible thinking and the other stances in a writer's mindset. (See Figure 5–10.)

Shifting the Language We Use in Writing Workshop

Principles to Promote	Instead of Saying . . .	Try Saying . . .
Writing and revision can be playful and fun—and shouldn't feel like drudgery.	"OK, everyone, it's time to get out your writing work."	"Let's try playing with some of these ideas in your writing and see where it takes you."
Writing often involves discovering what we think, not knowing all our ideas ahead of time.	"Remember to start with a thesis statement in your introduction to explain what you're going to say."	"I wonder what you might discover by writing about this topic."

Figure 5–10   Shifting the Language We Use in Writing Workshop   *(continues)*

(continued)

Shifting the Language We Use in Writing Workshop

Principles to Promote	Instead of Saying . . .	Try Saying . . .
Writing often involves discovering what we think, not knowing all our ideas ahead of time *(continued)*	"Make sure to finish your plan before you start your draft."	"Some writers map out ideas ahead of time with outlines, webs, or other prewriting. Others dive right in. Whatever you choose, try to be open to surprises."
	"Write what you know about ___."	"Write as quickly as you can about ___. You might find out something unexpected (a memory you'd forgotten, a feeling you didn't know you had, or a line you want to explore further)."
For students to invest in revision, they need to own the writing. They need choice, agency, and control, as much as possible—instead of formulas for writing to the demands of the teacher.	"Read carefully through my feedback to see areas that need revision."	"What do you think you might want to try to make your piece stronger?"
	"I think you should try a different lead."	"What if you try another lead or two and see what you come up with?"
	"I need you to go back and try ___ again."	"Here's a section you might want to focus on."

Shifting the Language We Use in Writing Workshop

Principles to Promote	Instead of Saying . . .	Try Saying . . .
Revision should be something students do willingly, because they care about their writing, not an obligatory step (revision for the sake of revision).	"You should always make several significant revisions before turning in your final draft."	"Are there revisions you could try in order to make your final draft even stronger? Consider making some meaningful changes that are important to you."
Revision isn't about neatening up drafts; it's about developing our ideas as fully and effectively as possible. It takes solid effort and often many attempts and iterations.	"Your rough draft is your 'sloppy copy.' Be ready to turn it in by Friday."	"Turn in your most current draft this Friday. I'm sure you'll make lots of changes after this latest draft, but try to develop your ideas as fully as you can this week."
Revision is sometimes confused with editing. When we lump these together, students think revision is about fixing mistakes instead of reshaping our ideas.	"Make sure to edit and revise your draft before you turn it in."	"Remember that revision and editing are both important, but they're very different. Focus most of your energy on revising—adding, cutting, moving, and changing parts of your writing so they match your vision for your piece."

(continues)

(continued)

Shifting the Language We Use in Writing Workshop

Principles to Promote	Instead of Saying . . .	Try Saying . . .
Revision is sometimes confused with editing. When we lump these together, students think revision is about fixing mistakes instead of reshaping our ideas, *(continued)*	"As you revise, hunt through your draft for things to fix."	"Don't worry about things like spelling and punctuation just yet—we'll get there later when we edit. For now, focus on things like clarity, voice, and meaning."
Authentic revision requires vulnerability and flexibility. These are lost when grades are the primary motivator. Instead, kids play it safe—or revise out of compulsion rather than intrinsic desire.	"Your process—including evidence of revision—is a big part of your grade, so make sure your final draft doesn't look like your first!"	"It's important to try new things and think flexibly as a writer, but this isn't easy. It's your choice what you decide to change. You won't be penalized for trying new approaches—in fact, it's encouraged. So, go for it!"
We want students to reflect on their own goals as writers and discover what strong writing means to them.	"Remember: you're supposed to be working on Standard 4.2: 'Write informative texts to examine a topic . . .'" "Keep checking out the 'I can' statements posted on the board."	"Remember to look back at the characteristics of effective informative writing that you brainstormed with classmates." "Think back at the goals you created for yourself as a writer. How are you meeting these so far?"

Shifting the Language We Use in Writing Workshop

Principles to Promote	Instead of Saying . . .	Try Saying . . .
Models and mentor texts can be helpful but limiting. Let students know that these can serve as guides, but kids don't have to be constrained by them.	"Be sure to follow the models and example pieces I've given you."	"Use the models if they help you. You can try something similar to those mentor texts, or you might branch out to something different."

Practice: Using Minilessons to Stretch Our Drafts—and Ourselves

Give your students plenty of opportunities to try new approaches and stretch themselves through your minilessons. You could ask them to take on different points of view, explore metaphorical thinking, follow their "wonderings," or play with unusual genres and formats.

Encourage different perspectives and contrarian ideas

One of the most powerful ways to promote flexible thinking is to ask students to step out of their own perspective or to take a position that runs counter to what's expected. Ask them to take an unexpected side for a debate or persuasive essay—or to try writing from a different point of view with a narrative or even an informational piece. Encouraging writers to shift away from their usual frame of reference can yield some wonderful surprises.

When Kathy was writing a biography about Amelia Earhart, she experimented by telling the aviator's story from the point of view of a longtime neighbor. Though Kathy's narrator was fictitious, the stories she recounted were true and well researched. By taking on this perspective, Kathy was able to share telling anecdotes and illuminate parts of Earhart's personality that we might not hear in a typical informational piece:

You want to know about Amelia Earhart? Well, she was born on July 24, 1897, in Atchison, Kansas—I know, 'cause she lived right down the street from me. I was there for her birth. Amelia was a feisty little thing, kickin' and screamin' an' all. She was so cute, with her little tufts of hair sticking out of her small head. . . .

For her ninth Christmas, her father gave her a .22 caliber Hamilton rifle, a rather unusual gift at the time, as girls were not supposed to like hunting, or sports, or anything like that. She had read an article about how the rats in Panama spread disease, and she worried the rats in Atchison might be doing the same. So, she rid her Grandmother Otis's barn of rats, and, sticking to the hunter's code, she left no creature to suffer (even if it meant she was late for dinner, much to her grandmother's scorn).

By writing from this point of view (rather than that of an objective, detached narrator), Kathy brought history alive. She presented Earhart's life through compelling stories, not as a typical list of biographical facts. Using different narrators meant Kathy could insert commentary about important events and personalize Earhart's role as a pioneering feminist:

One day, she and her father went to an air show at Long Beach. She took her first ride in an airplane then, with pilot Frank Hawk. In her letter, she told me, "By the time I had got two or three hundred feet off the ground, I knew I had to fly." She soon began taking flying lessons with a fellow female pilot, Neta Snook. It had to be another woman, as most men at the time would not teach women to fly.

Encourage your students to be flexible by writing not just *from* multiple perspectives but *to* different audiences than they might normally. In the spring of 2020 during the coronavirus pandemic, Emy wrote a letter directly to the virus:

Dear COVID-19,

Why do you have to trap the whole world away? Why do you have to take the lives of many innocent people? Why do people have to lose their jobs because of you? Why are you doing this? There are so many questions that we are all wondering, like, When will this be over? You are trapping us in our houses, or on a cruise ship, or in a hospital, like a jail, not letting us leave, like we did something wrong. You are emptying our cities, and taking away our happiness. . . .

Emy had a great idea and beginning, but she took it even further—by wondering what the coronavirus itself might say if it wrote back to us. This was a powerful shift in thinking that led to a companion piece to her first letter: a reply from the virus itself. Here's part of it:

Dear Humans,

Thank you for all of your wonderful questions, but you are making me sound like I'm such an awful thing. I just want to say, I'm doing my job: spreading, and taking over. I'm a virus. This is what a virus does.

To be honest, I think you needed more family time, too. By trapping you in your houses, it gives you that perfect opportunity . . . If you don't already know, I'm actually helping the environment. The pollution is definitely better, because you humans are now stuck at home, so stop complaining . . .

Sincerely,

COVID-19

This openness to different points of view and unexpected ideas led Emy to think about the quarantine through the cold, hard eyes of a virus.

Try metaphorical thinking

Many of us teach similes, metaphors, and personification to show strong, intentional word choice, but these do more than just add beautiful language. Metaphorical thinking helps us see with fresh eyes, particularly with a topic we thought we knew.

When I placed a variety of common objects on the desks in my classroom, I asked students to look at them in new ways, using figurative language. Molly described an unshelled peanut with metaphors—images that stay with me to this day when I'm cracking one open:

Peanut

A little brown bowling pin

A Russian nesting doll

A tiny maraca

An Easter egg

Hiding jelly beans within

When Michael wanted to capture a stapler, he gave it life:

It sleeps
with silver jaws.
Waking up
it stands with only one paw.
Jabs at paper
Stabs at walls
Reloads and laughs
as its fangs are replaced.

When Ulysses was describing his father's salt-and-pepper beard in a poem, he used a single, vivid metaphor:

Dad's beard
Swirling pine trees
All coated with snow
On a wintery night.

Many of us discuss figurative language when we teach poetry or narrative writing, but metaphorical thinking is part of every genre. It captures the subject of an essay or informational piece in novel ways—and often helps us understand a concept more deeply and clearly. When my students wrote signs about important natural and historical features around our town, they described our nearby estuary, with its strong tides, as a "mixing bowl bringing rich nutrients and an 'all-you-can-eat buffet' to many species." In another sign about gundalows—flat-bottomed boats indigenous to our local waterways—they wrote that they were "the tractor-trailers of their time," hauling timber and other goods along our rivers in the centuries before automobiles.

Ask your students to consider metaphors as a way to keep their thinking flexible, no matter what genre they're writing.

Ask "What if?" and "I wonder?"

Ask students to riff off two deceptively simple questions: "What if?" and "I wonder?" Have them reflect on a draft by rereading it and then asking themselves a series of "What if?" or "I wonder?" questions.

My student Sarah began a narrative by describing a favorite place—the wetland behind her house. As she remembered her times playing there, Sarah recalled being able to hear "the faint echo of trickling water" beneath her feet. Her piece took an exciting fictional turn once she began asking herself questions, like, "What if I found a waterfall beneath the ground? What if there was an underground cave or some sort of trap I fell into?" As she followed her wonderings, Sarah's piece took an interesting turn:

> This swamp always had its mysteries, whether they have already been seen or waiting to be discovered. The question of what had been hiding here lingered in my head as my shovel drew closer to the answer. . . . I hit roots on my way down, so I pried them away and kept digging. *How far down was this thing?* My hands began to strain as my grip tightened on the handle. My heart pumped excitement through my body, filling me with determination. I was almost there; I could feel it.
>
> That's when the dirt gave way.

Where would Sarah go next—Sarah the writer and Sarah the impromptu explorer? "What if there was an abandoned temple deep underground? What if it *wasn't* abandoned?" Because Sarah asked herself "What if?" and "I wonder?" questions like these, the thinking about her piece stayed pliable and her excitement grew.

Encourage play

Some of the best ways we can bolster flexible thinking is by encouraging play through unconventional forms (including blackout poems, six-word stories, memes, and found poems). Be open to these unusual genres, such as blackout poems. For these, students take a chunk of text (newspaper article or random page from a book), scan it for anchor words (interesting phrases or ideas packed with meaning), and eliminate the words they don't need—eventually removing the majority of the text and revealing something new. Like found poems, blackout poems help students discover new meaning in unexpected places. I collaborated with my social studies colleague to have our students create blackout poems by transforming the Bill of Rights and other founding documents (see Figure 5–11).

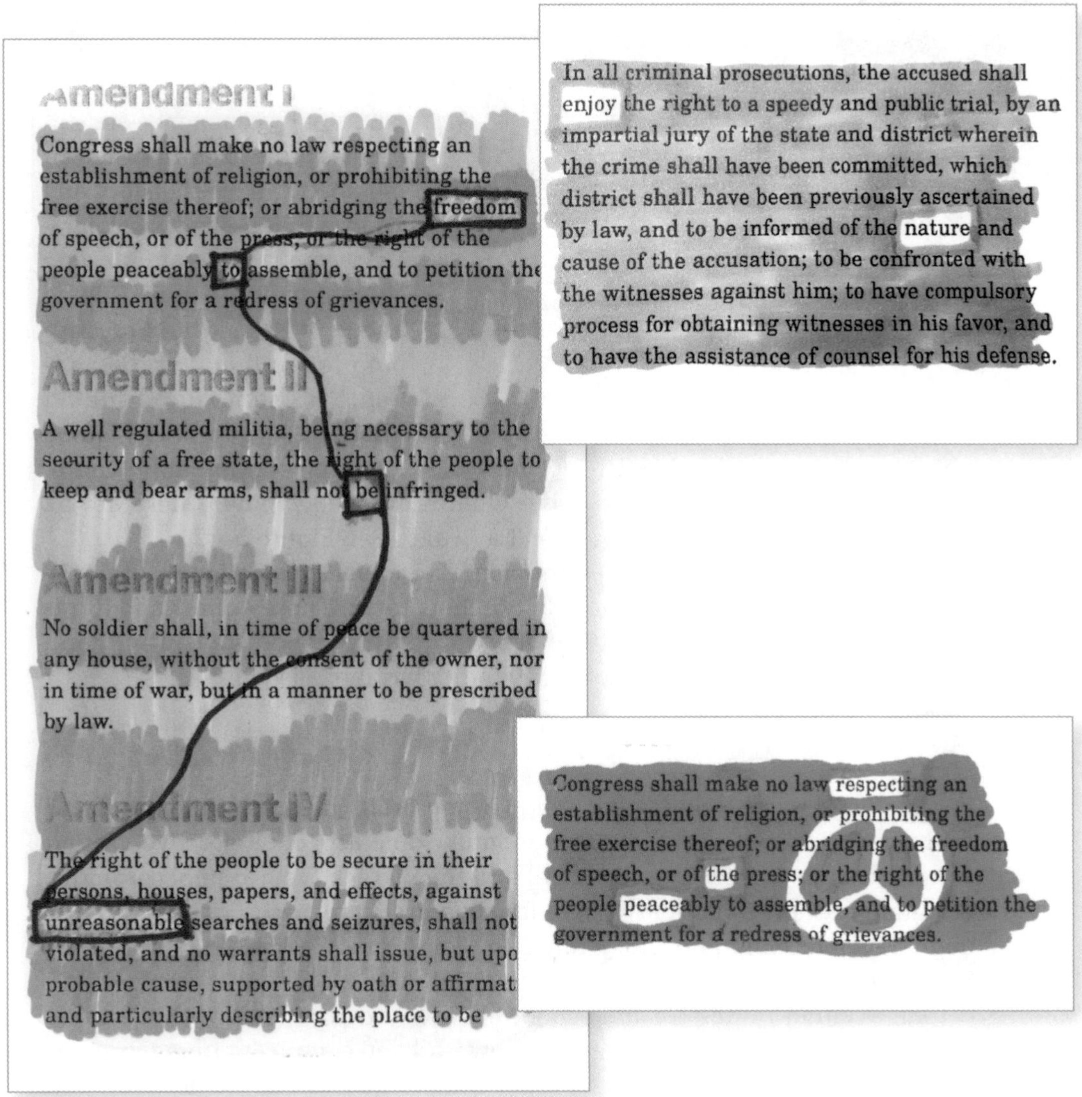

Figure 5–11   Blackout Poems

When there are 57 redcoats In your house but you aren't at war.

Figure 5–12 Memes are another example of a form that promote play.

Memes—those ubiquitous online creations that pair an image with humorous or provocative text—are another example of a form that promotes play. During the same civics collaboration with social studies, our eighth graders created memes about the events leading up to the Revolutionary War. With this new form—matching an unlikely picture with a pithy comment—our students synthesized their learning about Colonial history and presented it in whimsical, incisive ways. For example, one student took a popular meme image of Kermit the Frog sipping tea and added the caption, "It's so taxing drinking tea with such outrageous prices." Another repurposed a widespread meme image—a baby shaking his fist—to show the Colonists' outrage at having to house British soldiers (as part of the Quartering Act), "When there are 57 Redcoats in your house, but you aren't at war." (See Figure 5–12.)

New and alternate forms of expression, like memes, sometimes get pooh-poohed as less valid, but we shouldn't eschew them. These genres and forms nudge us to experiment (with brevity, wordplay, perspective shifting, and more)—and encourage us to do so with other writing, as well.

Wreck a draft

For this minilesson, writers take an emerging draft, idea, or mentor text, and turn it upside down. Have students identify some aspect of effective writing (a vivid description or engaging title) and then wreck their draft accordingly, rewriting to make it gloriously, *painfully* bad in that respect. For example, we might revel in coming up with a title like "The Time I Broke My Arm" or "My Scary Story" or take a sentence from our draft about a trivial moment (Eating cereal? Waiting in line for the school bus?) and overwrite it with dramatic flourish. Or we might take something powerful and significant from our piece (spotting a bear on a hike; a baby sister coming home from the hospital) and brush over it in the most cursory fashion.

How can we wreck a draft? First, brainstorm a list of ways as a class. Many of these will likely be tied to certain genres your students are familiar with (or are currently working on). Your class list might include items such as these:

- writing terrible titles (titles that are labels as opposed to intriguing invitations; titles that reveal too much or too little)

- beginning with uninviting leads (leads that summarize or explain rather than set a scene; boring snoozers without a hook)

- telling about *everything* or giving too little attention to important events or too much attention to trivial ones (for narrative writing)

- overloading with too many facts—or not enough (for informational writing)

- stating our opinion with no evidence—or never taking a firm stance (for persuasive writing)

The list could go on and on; just make sure the ideas come from students (otherwise they sound like a list of teacher pet peeves). It may go without saying, but be sure students wreck only their *own* drafts or ones from published mentor texts. (The difference is like watching a toddler's delight in knocking down their own tower of blocks versus their indignation at seeing someone else do it.) The point is *play*—to have fun messing with our own writing, knowing that we can return to our original draft after wreaking havoc on it.

Students get a laugh out of making their own terrible rewrites, but more importantly, in the process of wrecking a draft, they are thinking about the inverse: what makes writing strong and effective. By reflecting about what makes one draft awful—"I totally gave away my ending with my title" or "I took loads of time describing something that didn't matter to the story"—they're actually thinking about ways to improve their writing (their current piece and future ones). Pausing the drafting process briefly—and engaging in a little draft-destruction revelry—can help us to see our piece anew.

Note: Sometimes, in trying to wreck a draft, we actually stumble upon something great. For instance, students may say, "Titles shouldn't be too long," then reconsider when someone mentions an exception (*Alexander and the Terrible, Horrible, No Good, Very Bad Day*). Or they might say that "leads shouldn't give away too much," until someone points out the first lines of *Mick Harte Was Here*, which reveal the death of the narrator's brother straightaway ("Let me say right off the bat, it was a bike accident . . ." [Park 1995, 3]).

As we play with a draft, we sometimes bend the rules in wonderfully inventive ways. My student Eleanor added melodrama and an incongruous style with a narrative about a relatively mundane winter outing with her family:

> T'was early in the afternoon. . . . The outside world was a fury of white and cold. As we donned our outerwear I glanced around at my comrades. My little brother, not yet seven years of age, bravely pulling on his sturdy winter boots. My mother and father with their bulky coats steeling themselves for the dangerous journey ahead. Together we walked confidently to the door, our hubris getting the best of us, tricking us into believing that this would be an easy task. Oh, what fools we were!

As she described the short walk from the hotel to the bus shuttle with overblown language reminiscent of another era, we, her readers, couldn't help but laugh:

> The wicked snow was flying through the air in evil droves coming at us from every side. It was a relentless foe. We stopped, exhausted and heartbroken, resigned to our fate of eventually becoming part of the horrid, frozen landscape. . . .
> Then, lo! Our savior arrived in the form of a majestic white and blue hotel mini-bus! It was truly a glorious sight to behold!

Have your students try wrecking a draft, and see what emerges.

Practice: Publishing and Celebrating by Reflecting on a Draft's Evolution

Have students post their earliest drafts or quickwrites side by side with their completed (or almost-done) drafts. They can display these physically—on a large sheet of oaktag or classroom bulletin board, for example—or digitally, as part of an online portfolio.

After posting, ask students to reflect on the changes they notice. Have them highlight passages or sections that show the most significant revisions. They could place sticky notes to show where they tried new ideas (e.g., where they added new parts or tried different word choice). Like gazing at a living room wall of school photos—our framed pictures from primary grades up through senior year—we are taking note of what's grown and changed (our first-grade bowl cut transforming into feathered-back Farrah hair!). Of course, we should let students know that it's fine if they notice some similarities between the first and last drafts, if some features stay the same (like those same cute dimples that appear unchanged in our senior portrait!).

Have students write a brief writer's statement to accompany their drafts, answering these questions:

- What changes do you notice, from your earliest draft to your final (or nearly final) draft?

- Where were places that showed flexible thinking, where you tried something new?

- What did you try? Where did the idea come from?

- Are there lines or places in your draft that remained about the same? Why did you decide to keep these? What made them appealing as is?

Reflecting on a draft's evolution reinforces the importance of staying open to new ideas—and celebrates the changes we have made.

Keep the channel open.

—Martha Graham (de Mille 1991, 264)

It isn't easy staying flexible with our writing. It's natural when we get an idea for a draft to want to dash to the end, like runners locking our eyes on the finish-line ribbon. There's nothing wrong with our student writers finding a course and sticking to it, so long as they pick their heads up occasionally and realize there may be alternate routes they can take. Writing is less a highway road race and more of a cross-country ramble, with multiple potential paths and countless final destinations. We don't want our students to linger too long on the course, but the learning and fun are in keeping open to possibilities—in considering which route might be best for them.

6

Transfer

Writers Develop by Harnessing Learning from Past Experiences

For Hannah and the rest of my students, transfer was a time machine.

It was late in the school year, and my fifth graders and I decided to take it on the road to visit one of the elementary schools in our district to teach them what we had learned about revision. For many students, this was a return to their old K–4 hallways—in some cases, to their actual classrooms and teachers from two years earlier. We were armed with tools of the trade—sticky notes, markers, inspiring mentor texts, a slideshow presentation—and we were there to slow down the hot spot.

A few weeks earlier, I had asked my students, "If you could teach one revision strategy or approach to a class of third graders, what would it be? What helped you the most this year?" We discussed the skills and learning that had had the greatest impact on our writing over the past eight months: craft moves (like trying new leads, more vivid verbs, or dialogue) and revision processes (such as giving and receiving feedback). When someone mentioned, "Slow down the hot spot," heads started to nod.

When we arrived at Moharimet Elementary School, we were on a mission: to act as revision mentors, to teach students two grades below us how to focus on a few key places—hot spots—in our drafts. "They're like the most important or emotional moments in your writing," Phinn said, looking down at the scrum of wide-eyed third graders on the meeting rug, "but sometimes you breeze over them too fast."

"You can zoom in on these parts and make them stand out," Emma added. "It makes your story more exciting for readers because they feel like they are *there*, like you're giving them a movie in their minds."

Lauren cautioned that not every scene is a hot spot—that writers choose important or thrilling parts to slow down and take their time describing and pick other moments to jump through quickly. "It's like changing the tempo in a piece of music: it shakes up the listener and makes them pay attention."

With her third-grade sister sitting on the rug in front of her, Hannah shared an excerpt from her memoir "Stitches"—the before and after. "In my journal, I wrote a sentence that was kind of blah: 'I saw my sister trip and hit her head on the nightstand. She got stitches.' It was actually a really big and scary time for our family." Hannah glanced down at her sister, who nodded emphatically. "It sounded like a hot spot, so I zoomed in on it and slowed it down."

> When she sprinted into the room, she ran around the bed and tripped over the diaper bag. It was like I saw it in slow motion. Brooke lurching forward, smashing her face into the sharp corner of the nightstand. It happened in seconds. Her eyes growing wide, the air rushing past. For a second, I didn't know what just happened until she screamed. It was a high-pitched shriek. It rang out into the night for what seemed forever. It was only punctured by my parents' worried voices and some of my sister's cries. There was blood everywhere. It was on her chin and face, on the nightstand, everywhere! Suddenly, I heard my mom's quick and anxious voice, trying to calm Brooke down. "Brian! I'm going to take Brooke to the hospital, you watch the kids!"
>
> "Hannah! Move out of your mother's way!" And just like that, my mom and my sister were gone.

With my fifth graders' help, the third graders identified—and then tried—the different moves Hannah had used to capture this powerful memory:

Figure 6–1 Fifth Graders Talk with Third Graders as Revision Mentors

frame-by-frame details, thoughts, and dialogue. We chatted in small groups about our own drafts, tried new hot spots side by side with writing buddies, even started a whole-class story together. (See Figure 6–1.)

My fifth graders had come to teach younger students what they knew, but as we did so, we were deepening our own understanding. One of my students, Rose, put it this way: "Teaching them helped me, because even though I knew how to slow down the hot spots, I think I learned more by teaching them."

Part of being in a writer's mindset is being aware of the skills we bring to the page (or those we bring to an elementary classroom). When we do this, we are taking our know-how—the content knowledge and skills we've gleaned in the past—and intentionally applying these to new situations, to new pieces. Transfer doesn't have to be as involved as a revision mentor lesson; it's often just a moment of reflection as we're writing. When we plunge into a draft or hit a roadblock, we think, "This reminds me of . . . ," or "This is like the time when . . . ," or "I could try. . . ." In doing so, we call forth a trove of mental resources—whether we're drawing from minilessons we've been taught, books from favorite authors, techniques noticed in our peers' writing, or self-discoveries from our own previous pieces.

So how do we take stock of our writing knowledge and skills and transfer them? (See Figure 6–2.)

Belief: Writers Need to Look Back to Move Forward

When my students step into the classroom at the beginning of the year, I try to get a sense of what they know about strong writing. I ask them about the writing moves and revision strategies they already know and have used. At first, I often get blank expressions and responses like Justin's. "I don't really know," he wrote on his writing survey in early September (see Figure 6–3).

Figure 6–2 Transfer

Figure 6–3 Justin's Survey

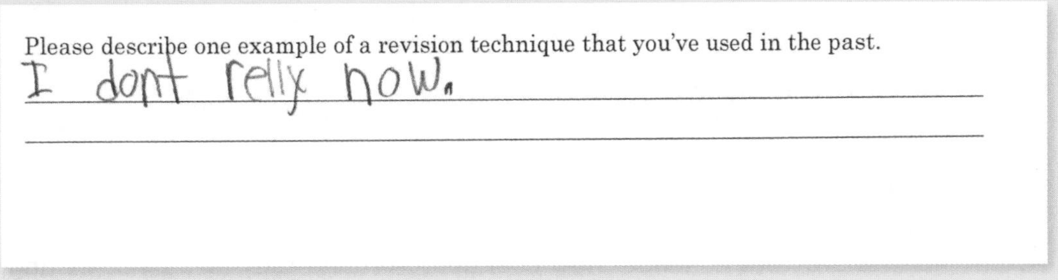

Please describe one example of a revision technique that you've used in the past.

I dont relly now.

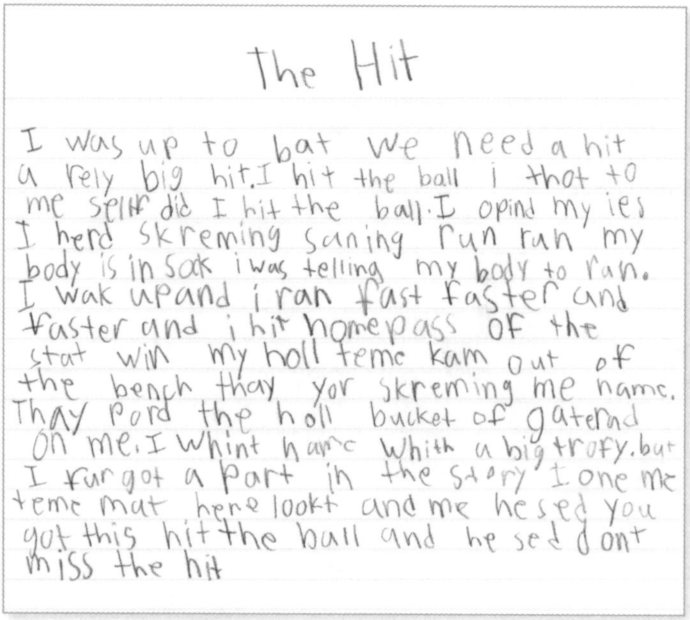

The Hit

I was up to bat we need a hit a rely big hit. I hit the ball i thot to me selff did I hit the ball. I opind my ies I herd skreming saning run run my body is in sock i was telling my body to ran. I wak upand i ran fast faster and faster and i hit homepass of the stat win my holl teme kam out of the bench thay yor skreming me name. Thay pord the holl bucket of gaternd on me. I whint hamc whith a big trofy. but I furgot a part in the story I one me teme mat here lookt and me he sed you got this hit the ball and he sed dont miss the hit

Figure 6–4 "The Hit"

But Justin *did* know lots about effective writing—and he came to my class with many skills, even if he wasn't aware of them. In one of his first pieces of the year, he wrote about a pivotal moment when he was up at bat for his baseball team (see Figure 6–4).

Justin's draft, though still emerging, had so much already. Bits of nice repetition ("We needed a hit, a really big hit."). Internal monologue ("I thought to myself, 'Did I hit the ball?'"). Dialogue ("I heard screaming, saying, 'Run, run!'"). A stretching out of time, a description of how it felt moment by moment ("My body was in shock. I was telling my body to run. I woke up and ran fast. Faster and faster."). Justin came to me with these strengths, but he couldn't see them yet.

Our students often know more—and are capable of more—than they think. It's hard to transfer skills and knowledge when we aren't even aware we have them, so, as teachers, we can help our students be cognizant of what they can do and what they already know about good writing. We can build this awareness by having students look back at writing pieces they know—by mining their own drafts, their classmates' writing, and the books and texts they love.

Practice: Setting Up Your Workshop by Reviewing Your Skill Set

Ask your students some version of these questions as you start off your year together: "What makes a piece of writing strong? What do you already know about good writing?" Have them brainstorm lists in their journals of their existing writing knowledge and skills. Share these in groups or with the whole class. Doing so reinforces the idea that students aren't some blank slates when they arrive, that no matter how confident—or not—they feel about writing, they bring valuable experiences and know-how to the table. Some students may describe things they learned in school or give answers that they think are "correct" (e.g., "Writing should have no spelling mistakes and be neat."), but many times their responses reveal unexpected observations ("I like it when it sounds like the author is talking right to me.").

Book Bistro

Sometimes these brainstorms can fall flat though; accessing and articulating what they know about writing is easy for some but challenging for others. To spark ideas, have students anchor this brainstorming in a specific artifact: a favorite book or piece of their own writing.

I often hold a Book Bistro in the first couple of weeks of school, asking each student to bring in a favorite book from the previous school year (or from any time in their lives). We make it festive, with food and music, and each of us shares the following:

- a short excerpt from the book—a passage with writing we love;

- an explanation of why this passage stood out; and

- a brief author promo—a description about this author's writing style (what makes their writing so enjoyable and distinctive). (See Figure 6–5.)

Figure 6–5   Hannah and Sarah Share During Our Book Bistro

As we showcase the books and authors we revere, we often realize we know more about effective writing than we thought. (See Figures 6–6 and 6–7.) During the Book Bistro, you will overhear comments like these:

- "Rick Riordan writes titles and first lines that hit you; like, they stop you in your tracks because they're strange and shocking. 'I Accidentally Vaporize My Pre-Algebra Teacher'—that's Chapter 1! Sometimes he puts in paragraphs that are just one sentence like that. He often writes like he's talking to *you*, the reader."

- "In *Schooled*, Gordon Korman has each chapter be narrated by a different character from the book. It's cool because there's Cap (a home-schooled hippie) in one, and Zach (a middle school bully-jerk) in another."

- "Kwame Alexander tells a whole story of these two brothers who love basketball, but the chapters are actually poems that don't rhyme."

- "I love the way Roald Dahl makes the BFG talk. It's so funny the way he speaks—like the way he calls the kids 'chidlers' and invents words like 'whizzpopper' for farts."

Figure 6–6   Mairtin and Dylan Share During Our Book Bistro

Figure 6–7   Cohen and Justin Share During Our Book Bistro

The Book Bistro starts with observations like these—specific to particular texts and authors—but we wrap up by creating lists of what these show us about effective writing in general.

I ask: "What do we know about good writing from these books? What are some things our favorite writers do?" Have students create a list of writing moves their favorite authors use, based on the book excerpts they brought in, like this:

As writers, we can:

- use shocking first lines that hit readers like a punch

- try unusual titles that grab readers' attention

- have a mix of paragraph lengths—sometimes just a single-sentence paragraph

- talk to our readers directly (the "you" voice)

- write about the same event from different points of view

- tell stories in verse or poetry

- write poems that don't rhyme

- use dialogue and talking that sounds like real characters (and the unusual ways they speak).

With an activity like the Book Bistro, we're building excitement for independent reading, but we're also accessing what we know about wonderful writing.

Flashback Showcase

A different twist on the beginning-of-the-year Book Bistro is the Flashback Showcase, where students bring in a piece of their own past writing that they're proud of. As with the Book Bistro, ask students to share the following in table groups:

- a short excerpt from their own writing piece

- an explanation of why this passage stood out—and why they chose this piece of writing overall

- a reflection on the writing moves and strategies that made their piece strong (Ask: "What are some things you tried as a writer with this piece? What specifically made this an effective piece of writing in your mind?")

- a reflection on their writing process (Ask: "What helped you as a writer on this piece—or any piece of writing? What helped you improve this draft—or any draft?")

These last questions broaden our students' thinking beyond stylistic and craft moves to include what they know about revision. Their lists often include reflections and personal idiosyncrasies about their own writing process (see Figure 6–8).

Here's how some students answered the question *What helped you improve this draft (or any draft)?*

It helped me to get feedback from a small group because I didn't feel comfortable sharing in a big group.

Using more juicy words.

I did a ton of conferences with teachers, friends, and even brought it home to read to my dog.

It helps me to draw pictures first.

I read it over to myself to make sure it sounds right.

I try to put an image in my head and see if the next image makes sense to the one before.

It helps when I sit in groups and people give me suggestions because then I get more stuff to write.

Figure 6–8   What Helps You as a Writer?

Keep in mind: When students discuss a piece of their own past writing, they sometimes fixate on its imperfections. As they get a bit older, they tend to dismiss or disparage their writing from earlier years. Remind them, though, that the point is to train our eyes on the positive: *What writing moves and strengths does this piece show? What can we learn about effective writing from it?*

Practice: Ending Your Year with Revision Videos or Revision Mentors

Bookend the year with the way you began—by reflecting on what we know about strong writing. These practices raise the bar though: they have us teach what we know to others.

Start with a (seemingly) simple question and invitation to your students: "What revision strategy or writing move has helped you the most this year? How might you teach this to others?" Then have them respond through revision videos or as revision mentors.

Revision Videos

With Revision Videos, students use screencasting software (such as Screencastify) to explain what made the biggest impact on their writing. They create a minilesson by storyboarding their ideas, designing a slideshow (using PowerPoint or Google Slides), and crafting a voice-over script of their writing tips and suggestions.

Start by asking students to reflect on their year of writing and experimenting together. *What improved their writing the most? What reminders could they give to other writers through their videos? What could they teach next year's students in your classroom?* (See Figure 6–9.)

Revision Video Process

In their revision videos, have students do the following:

▸ *name and explain the writing move or revision strategy* that influenced them most (e.g., explaining what a lead is; see Figure 6–10)

▸ *describe why the craft move or strategy is helpful,* why it makes our writing better (e.g., describing how a strong lead can pull in readers and gives them a window into the story)

▸ *show others how* to do it (e.g., show different types of leads writers can use; see Figure 6–11)

▸ *give examples* from their own writing or other authors (e.g., sentences showing a draft before and after using the move or strategy)

▸ *add tips or caveats* to keep in mind (e.g., "Never throw away a good lead—you could use it somewhere else in your story!")

▸ *make it interactive*—give viewers a chance to try it (e.g., asking listeners to pause the video and try a new lead to a sample draft)

Figure 6–9 Revision Video Process

I allow students to work alone or in pairs on this project, and it motivates them—even in the waning days of school in June—when they know they're creating a lesson that will be used with my future fifth graders (and I *do* use them). Since I give them choice, their videos cover a range of topics: writing engaging titles; using vivid verbs; adding sensory details; getting feedback from peers; adding thoughts and feelings; and more (see Figures 6–10 through 6–12).

Revision Mentors

Another way for students to teach what they know about writing is with Revision Mentors. Have your students act as revision mentors for a younger class (as I described in the chapter opening) or even for their own classmates. When my fifth graders visited third graders in another school in our district, we collaborated on a common minilesson—slowing down the hot spot (see Figure 6–13). Try something similar, or perhaps place students in mentor pairs or small groups—akin to reading buddies—allowing them to teach minilessons of their own to their partners.

Instead of you, the teacher, deciding what writing skill to have mentors teach, ask your students to decide. Start by having them do a brief revision retrospective—a reflection on what strategy or move improved their writing

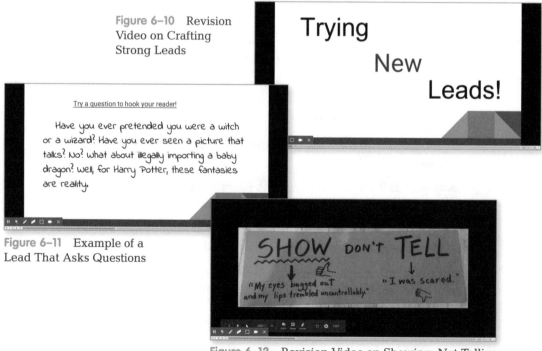

Figure 6–10 Revision Video on Crafting Strong Leads

Figure 6–11 Example of a Lead That Asks Questions

Figure 6–12 Revision Video on Showing, Not Telling

Figure 6–13   Revision Mentors Visit with Third Graders

the most over the course of the year. (See Figures 6–14 and 6–15.) Next, plan a mentor lesson either as whole class or in small groups. (See Figure 6–16.)

Why try Revision Mentors (or Revision Videos)? When we're teaching others, we're actually reteaching ourselves. One of the third graders told his teacher after our visit, "I learned something new to make my writing better, and you know what? I think those fifth graders learned a lot, too, by talking with us." (See Figure 6–19.)

Mentoring and teaching builds transfer for several reasons:

- When writers consider what's helped them the most, they are relearning these lessons more deeply, circling back to knowledge and skills in new ways. Here's how my student Ulysses put it: "Teaching helped me as a writer because you have to understand what you are talking about in order to explain it."

Figure 6–14   Rose's Revision Retrospective

Name: Rose,   Date: 5-21

Revision Retrospective!

(retro = back; spect = look/see…So, looking back at our year of revisions)

Dear Antelopes,

    As you think back to all the revision strategies we've learned and practiced this year, which one has helped you the most to improve your writing? **In the space below, please tell me which strategy has been most useful and why/how it has helped you as a writer:**

I think one thing that was useful was making a movie in my mind also slowing down the hotspot because those things are sort of simular. I think they help because instead of saying just, "im mad," you might tell what you look like, like "my face is burning red, and my eyes are squinty." So I think it makes the story better. So I think it would be good to tell the 2nd graders about it.

Figure 6–15   Liam's Revision Retrospective

Revision Retrospective!

(retro = back; spect = look/see…So, looking back at our year of revisions)

Dear Antelopes,

    As you think back to all the revision strategies we've learned and practiced this year, which one has helped you the most to improve your writing? **In the space below, please tell me which strategy has been most useful and why/how it has helped you as a writer:**

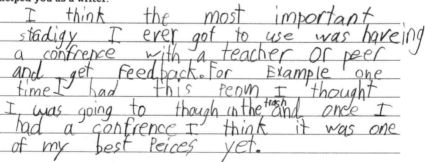

I think the most important stadigy I ever got to use was haveing a confrence with a teacher or peer and get feedback. For Example one time I had this peom I thought I was going to though in the trash and once I had a confrence I think it was one of my best peices yet.

- As any educator knows, as we plan how to teach a skill, we have to break down its steps, consider it from all angles, apply it to different situations. As Haley, another one of my students, said, "To teach something, you need to know it really well."

- When we see our students'—or mentees'—reactions in real time, we learn even more. "When the third graders started asking questions, I really thought about our hot spots in a new way," Courtney said.

- Lastly, as we prepare a lesson, we see our own writing anew, often recognizing how much we've grown. According to Gabi, "It showed me where I was in third grade—and then looking at my piece, it showed how I have improved as a writer."

Revision Mentors

As your students plan their mentor lessons, remind them to do the following:

▶ *Explain the move or skill in grade-appropriate language—and share why it improves our writing.* **With the third graders, we explained how some parts of a story are in our head but may not be on the page yet. We discussed how when we slow down a hot spot as writers, it's like we're turning a "magic camera" at those important moments and zooming in on them to make the scenes come alive.**

▶ *Provide examples of the craft move or strategy that are tailored to their mentees.* **We looked for examples of hot spots in the novel the third graders were reading aloud:** *Where the Mountain Meets the Moon,* **by Grace Lin.**

▶ *Show how to use the move, giving mentees opportunities for guided and independent practice.* **With the third graders, we took a class story they were already writing—about a group of kids bike riding through an impending lightning storm—and discussed possible hot spots to develop. Working in small groups together, the fifth and third graders wrote lines they could add to the story (using dialogue, sensory details, or thoughts; see Figure 6–17). Later, we took time to try hot spots independently, writing alongside each other—starting new hot spots of our own or adding ones to an existing story (see Figure 6–18).**

Figure 6–16   Revision Mentors

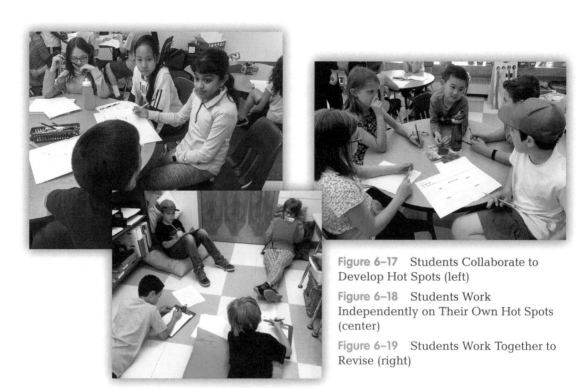

Figure 6–17   Students Collaborate to Develop Hot Spots (left)

Figure 6–18   Students Work Independently on Their Own Hot Spots (center)

Figure 6–19   Students Work Together to Revise (right)

Whether you use Revision Mentors, Revision Videos, or some other format, there is no better vehicle for transfer than teaching a skill to others. As we search for ways to explain a craft move or revision strategy to a new audience, we are rediscovering its importance and bonding it to ourselves for the long haul. You can see what some of my students thought about this activity in Figure 6–20.

> Maybe teaching other people stuff could help you because to be able to teach something you need to know it really well. Also you could get new ideas from listening to other people.

> ReVision Mentor Reflections 185
> Teaching helped me as a writer because you have to understand what you are talking about in order to explain it. I thought the 3rd graders seemed to get the adding more detail part because my brother had a part in his story about lava dripping down his leg.

> I Think teaching could help you because you get to see how much you've grown as a writer

> I think if You teach some one some thing, it will help You understand it more.

Figure 6–20   Student Reflections on Revision Mentors

Belief: Writers Need to Take Laps and Spiral Back to Practice

Nothing takes the wind out of our teaching sails like a student who seems to forget what they already learned. It's deflating when students approach a piece of writing like it's the first time—when they seem to ignore the titles lesson they grasped just last month or when they neglect all semblance of conventions that you'd swear they had a handle on. They suddenly turn in a draft titled "My Story" or a narrative completely devoid of paragraphing and you think, "Not only did I teach them this, but I saw them *master* it!"

But skills and knowledge don't just automatically stick. When we learn a new skill in a sport—say, a slice serve in tennis—we don't expect to try it once and then have it *down*. We learn the motions—how to grip the handle, rotate our body, strike across the ball—and then practice them repeatedly until they become motor memory. Eventually these moves become part of our repertoire of shots, but it takes time, rehearsal, and practice.

Writers need the same opportunities to spiral back, to try skills repeatedly but with increasing complexity—to (in the words of Kelly Gallagher and Penny Kittle) take "laps" with our learning (2018, 140).

We also need chances to consider how to repurpose the skills we have, to adapt them to different situations. So we know how to serve a ball with spin, but when might we use it in a new match, with a different competitor? When we transfer a skill, we consciously consider how we could employ it for a fresh purpose or context (maybe against an opponent with a shaky backhand or to set up an approach to the net).

As teachers, we can help by pausing occasionally during the year and asking our students to (1) add to their growing list of writing skills and knowledge and (2) consider how to reuse and adapt these to new pieces and genres.

Practice: Drafting by Spiraling Back to Our Skills

That list you had students brainstorm in the first weeks of school—*What makes a piece of writing strong?*—shouldn't stay static. What our students know and can do on week one will undoubtedly change as they have enriching writing and reading experiences.

As your writers learn new skills, it helps them to have a visual reminder of what's in their quiver. Nancie Atwell (1998) asks her students to keep track of the proofreading skills they know in a personalized editing checklist, a list they continually update as their learning grows (252–53). For this practice, ask your students what *revision* skills they know—which qualities and moves make for a great piece of writing. As teachers, many of us post writing strategies and skills we've taught up on our walls, which is fine, but the power is in students keeping their own lists, in their own words, and referring back to them.

So circle back. Pause periodically throughout the year and ask students to make an update. (See Figure 6–21.)

For example, as we began a poetry unit one winter, I asked my fifth graders, including Miles, what they had learned about effective writing that they might bring to their poems. He added the following strategies to his list:

- "Stretch out time." On his list, Miles recalled how he, as a writer, knew how to focus in on certain key moments and play with time (something he gleaned when we wrote personal narratives in the fall).

- "Keep my readers guessing." Miles had read and loved riddle poems—poems with extended metaphors from the likes of Valerie Worth and Charles Simic—where the subject was removed (be it dandelion or watermelon), forcing us to make guesses. He knew writers sometimes keep readers in the dark before they reveal something big at the end.

- "Hook readers in the lead."

- "Give out clues, but don't give everything away."

By taking a few moments to reflect back on his learning, Miles adapted these and other skills for a free-verse poem he was writing about an unusual race. His poem began with an intriguing, dramatic lead that sounded like a Wild West showdown:

> The door squeaked open
>
> he hopped in,
>
> the door closed
>
> it was just us now

Miles dropped clues and added mystery, with an ominous feel (as he had noticed other writers doing during read-alouds throughout the year):

> We sat there
>
> staring at each other,
>
> he twitched his cheek,
>
> he took deep, menacing breaths

Drafting by Spiraling Back to Our Skills

Have students add to their "What makes a piece of writing strong?" lists. Ask: "Have we learned anything new about effective writing that we could add to our lists?" You might try this activity after:

▶ you've led a minilesson that resonated with them,

▶ they've listened to an inspiring read-aloud, or

▶ they've read each other's work.

Also have students reflect and refer back to their lists before writing a new piece of writing or genre. When you do, ask: "Is there anything from your list that you might use with this new piece of writing? How could you try it? How might you have to adapt this skill for this new draft or genre?"

Keep these reflections brief—just enough to kick-start students' transfer. You might try this as:

▶ a student self-reflection (e.g., a beginning-of-class bell ringer before starting a new draft),

▶ a turn-and-talk with a partner, or

▶ a whole-class discussion.

Figure 6–21   Drafting by Spiraling Back to Our Skills

He used pacing, slowed down time, and turned his writer's camera to a few key details (as he had done with his memoir early in the year):

I got up out of my seat,

we got in ready position,

his ears back,

my eyes fixed on the door

In our minds we counted,

1 . . . 2 . . . 3 . . . GO,

We sped off,

him in the lead,

I tried to catch up to him,

But it was no use,

his paws gripped the ground and

pushed him off into the lead

Miles ended with a bit of humor and the big reveal—the identity of his racing competitor:

The next thing you know

he had won.

No surprise.

I had been beaten by a four-legged animal . . .

a cat.

By reflecting on his own repertoire of "shots," Miles spiraled back and transferred the writing skills in his notebook to a new poem, a new context.

Belief: Reading Like a Writer Builds Transfer

"'The focus on my artistic life has been trying to learn to write emotionally moving stories that a reader feels compelled to finish,'" the writer and teacher George Saunders says (Sehgal 2021). To write stories like this—and teach his university students to do so as well—he studies his idols. In his book *A Swim in the Pond in the Rain*, Saunders analyzes—affectionately, reverently—the small but significant decisions of some of his favorite Russian short story writers from the nineteenth century. The purpose of his book, he says, is "diagnostic": "'If a story drew us in, kept us reading, made us feel respected, how did it do that?'" (Sehgal 2021).

How did they do that? We may not tackle Tolstoy with our students, but that's the question to be asking when we're reading like writers.

In general, our students relish reading for the joys of the story—and they should. Perhaps we're reading aloud to them, watching their reactions as they are riveted to the action—or maybe they're nestled in a corner on a carpet square, engrossed in a novel of their own. Whether it's an individual or a communal act, it's a treat when we immerse ourselves as readers, inhabiting a mysterious world, confronting bullies far from home, or fighting for survival vicariously. And we want our students in this reading zone—in the flow of reading—most of the time.

But sometimes we need to ask them to make an important shift: to read like writers. On occasion, we should ask our students to pay attention to the writer's craft, whether the writer is a published author or peer—to tune their eyes and ears to the lines they want to emulate. We can mine our mentors for their signature moves and patterns; we can consider how their decisions on the page pulled us in, made us smile, left a mark. When we read like writers, we're identifying the author's moves, breaking down how they're done, thinking about their effect. These are key steps—all of them—when we're trying to transfer a skill from something we've *read* to something we're *writing*.

Practice: Using Read-Alouds to Foster Transfer

When you—or more importantly, your students—take delight in an author's craft during a read-aloud, take some time to build transfer into the equation. For example, when I read *Booked*, by Kwame Alexander (2016), students love the scene when the main character, Nick, is daydreaming about being a soccer star, only to get called out by his teacher. In the middle of eighth-grade English class, Nick is imagining himself about to make the game-winning kick, the crowd roaring his name:

> It's 3–3.
>
> Your turn
>
> to rev the engine,
>
> turn on the jets.
>
> Score, and you win. (13)

In the midst of this dreamscape, Nick's real world comes crashing in:

> Ms. Hardwick
>
> streaks across the field
>
> in her heels and
>
> purple polyester dress
>
> yelling:
>
> NICHOLAS HALL,
>
> PAY
>
> ATTENTION! (14)

I don't want to interrupt the flow of the story just then, but, noting their chuckles and smiles, I decide to return to that passage a day or two later. "I remember you loved the part when Nick gets busted by Mrs. Hardwick. Let's reread that part. . . . What did you notice Kwame Alexander did there?" Students' hands shoot up. Students share responses such as these:

- "He's writing it like he's talking to us. He saying 'you,' like 'Score, and you win' and the crowd 'screams your name.'"

- "It like how he puts us right into the story—like we're living in it, in Nick's mind, as he's dreaming about playing for Barcelona."

- "We can relate to it. . . . A lot of us dream about playing professional sports."

- "It's funny when his teacher catches him not paying attention. I've definitely seen that happen in class."

In just a short aside, my students have identified lots of Alexander's moves—some that I anticipated, some that I didn't. I roll with the conversation, highlighting the moves they mention, helping them give a name to some (e.g., second-person narration). I keep the discussion moving, asking questions that help them think like writers and spark some transfer. (See Figure 6–22.)

For students like Jason, conversations like these can have a huge impact. Jason wanted to write a piece about how teenagers like him get so engrossed in playing video games or binge-watching TV shows that they lose all sense of time. Experimenting with the second person—just as Kwame Alexander did—made all the difference.

Jason wanted to capture an experience that was both personal and relatable: the moment "you" come out of the daze of the screen and realize you've been at it for hours and it's nearly dawn—and your parents will *kill* you if they find out:

You're beginning to freak out, so you remember all the creaky spots in your hardwood floor—the house is like 2,000 years old—and you start run-lunging from non-creaky spot to non-creaky spot until you finally make it to the stairs. So, you tiptoe up the stairs and you make it to your bed. Just as you fall in bed and get wrapped up, you hear your parents walking down the hallway, and then your head starts to spin faster than the earth. *Did I turn everything off? Did I turn the volume back? Are they going to know I was down there? AM I GOING TO GET GROUNDED?!?!*

Jason's decision to try the "you" voice—a move introduced during a read-aloud—catapulted his piece. Just as it did for Kwame Alexander's writing, it made Jason's piece relatable and funny, as if he were saying to readers, "We've all gone through something like this, haven't we?" There's humorous internal monologue ("AM I GOING TO GET GROUNDED?!"), hyperbole (the two-thousand-year-old house), and an almost stream-of-consciousness style. The writing was all Jason, but the moves were inspired by a read-aloud.

When trying this technique, keep the following pointers in mind:

- Use reading like a writer sparingly. Be judicious about when to stop the flow of the narrative and when to just savor reading for its sake. Be careful with the text, that you're not (in the words of poet Billy Collins) "beating it with a hose" to get it to reveal its secrets (1988, 58). We want students to feel a sense of discovery and agency—*Here's a move I could try*—but not at the expense of torturing the reading experience by grinding it to a halt.

- Take cues from the students. If they're interested in discussing an author's writing and excited to try it, you'll know. Does scrutinizing the magician's sleight of hand in order to figure out his trick ruin the fun? Not if we're an apprentice in the audience, honing our craft.

- The mentor text you use can be a published book, but you can also use a student's final draft or a piece of your own.

Read Like Writers to Foster Transfer

As you read like writers, try asking:

▸ What did you notice the author did here? What could we call this move?

▸ Why did this make the writing strong, or what did it do to us as readers? What did we love about it?

▸ How did the author do this? Let's figure it out. . . .

▸ How might we try it ourselves?

Figure 6–22   Read like Writers to Foster Transfer

Practice: Having Students Create a Rubric

I used to start a new writing unit—say, memoir—by dutifully posting the standards and "I can" statements on the board. *This is what a personal narrative looks like. These are its characteristics. This is what you'll be able to do at the end of this unit.* My neat bullet points on the whiteboard declared it, but that didn't mean my students were internalizing the skills.

We shouldn't keep these expectations hidden from students, but the power—and transfer—is when they discover them for themselves.

When you take on a common writing task or genre as a class, instead of handing out a rubric or list of criteria, put the task in students' hands. (See Figure 6–23.)

Here are a few things to keep in mind as they do this work:

- Let the words students use to describe strong writing be their own. Your students will likely borrow some of the language you, or other teachers, have used. (For example, "speaker tags" in the list in Figure 6–24 is something my class had heard me use to name the descriptors that accompany dialogue, such as "she asked" or "he said, scowling at his sister"). But the more they articulate craft moves in their words, the more they're likely to use them. When

Have Students Create the Rubric

▶ Find several strong models in the genre your students will be writing. The mentor texts might be from published authors or—even better—from students (perhaps examples from your previous years' writers).

▶ Ask: "What do you notice about these pieces? What makes them strong? What characteristics or qualities do they have in common?"

▶ As students work in small groups, have them read the texts like writers and then discuss the features and commonalities they noticed.

▶ Have groups share out their findings, and create a class list of characteristics—a class rubric for the writing piece they're about to begin.

Figure 6-23   Have Students Create the Rubric

you come together to create a single class rubric, keep as much of the student-generated descriptions as you can. The more it sounds like your students, the more they'll own it.

- Point out the connections and commonalities between different students' lists. For example, Will's group wrote, "P3D" (explaining that, in an effective memoir, readers can "picture everything in 3D"). Lea's group mentioned that strong writing "makes a movie in your head." During our discussion, I pointed out that both groups were discussing a similar characteristic—that narrative writing should create vivid, clear images in our minds as readers.
- The rubric may be student-centered, but, as the teacher, you're not a passive observer; you can certainly suggest important items that they might have overlooked. In Figure 6–24, the group includes a suggestion directly from me: answering the "So what?" question (i.e., how memoir writers show the significance of the event they're recounting).
- Highlight the most important characteristics students raise during the discussion, but don't get hung up on everyone having a perfect, identical list after the fact. Yes, you will meld together the groups' ideas into a single class list (on the board and likely a handout), but it's the *process* that matters. The discoveries for students happen while they are reading and talking with one another about effective writing. It may feel important to us, the teachers, to do some wordsmithery to the final rubric after class, but the learning for students is in the *during* and *doing*.

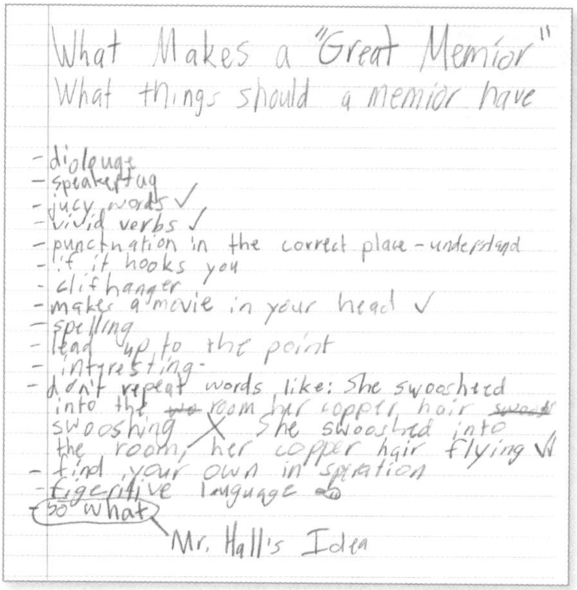
What Makes a "Great Memoir"
What things should a memoir have

- dialouge
- speaker tag
- jucy words ✓
- vivid verbs ✓
- punctuation in the correct place - understand
- if it hooks you
- clif hanger
- makes a movie in your head ✓
- spelling
- lead up to the point
- intresting
- don't repeat words like: She swooshed into the ~~ro~~ room her copper hair ~~swoosh~~ swooshing X She swooshed into the room, her copper hair flying ✓
- find your own inspiration
- figerative language
- so what

Mr. Hall's Idea

Figure 6–24 A Student's List of Characteristics That Make a Memoir Great

When students tease out the moves from mentor texts and create the rubric themselves, they're taking a much more active stance than they would if they just got handed a list of teacher expectations or Common Core jargon. They own it—and begin to transfer it—because they've made it themselves.

What's Your Takeaway?

Ask:

- **What line(s) do you wish you had written?**
- **What was something you noticed about your classmate's piece that you could use?**
- **Where might you try it?**

Figure 6–25 What's Your Takeaway?

Practice: Peer Conferring by Asking, "What's *Your* Takeaway?"

When our students confer with one another, it's generally thought of as a one-way windfall—comments given from readers to writer, in order to improve the draft. Feedback *is* a gift to the writer, but it benefits the audience as well.

In this conferring approach, rather than have your students give comments to the writer, have readers identify a writing move *they* want to take away and use for themselves. Ask readers what they appreciated about a peer's draft and what they might borrow for themselves as writers. (See Figure 6–25.)

When students think about their own takeaways, they might file them away for the future or use them straight off. For Ulysses, his takeaway filled an immediate need.

We were creating informational pieces about our local watershed area, Great Bay, and Ulysses struggled for a way to begin. He was writing about an event in the 1970s when Aristotle Onassis, an oil magnate, was planning to build a refinery on the shores near our town. Hatched in secret during the oil crisis, Onassis' plan nearly worked—and would have devastated the ecology of our area—if local activists hadn't rallied to stop it. Ulysses knew the history, and his writing had the facts, but it felt stale.

During a peer conference, he listened as another group read their draft about wastewater's effects on the bay. Their piece began:

> What's in your pee, and does it really go into Great Bay?!

The group went on to address how nitrogen (partly through human waste) was damaging our estuary, presenting their information in a compelling way.

After listening, Ulysses' takeaway was that "they started with a question, which pulled [him] in, and then they gave facts like it was mystery—like a problem for us to solve."

The moves Ulysses noticed helped transform his own draft. He revised, using a question as a hook and then teasing out details like a mystery novel unfolding:

> Did you know that a small conversation between two people could have changed Durham forever? It all started with a black Cadillac pulling up to a woman's house on Durham Point. The mysterious Realtor went up to the woman's house and asked how much he could offer her, but the woman said her land wasn't for sale. . . . The Realtor kept knocking on other doors asking the same question, and giving reasons why he wanted to buy it: for a golf course, for a family estate, for a wildlife preserve. The Realtor was actually asking for someone far, far away, and none of the reasons he said were true. He was actually working for one of the richest people in the world: Aristotle Onassis.

Transfer happens like this: when writers mine a bit of precious ore from somewhere else—a classmate's draft, a mentor text, their own past writing—and fashion it into a treasure of their own.

Chapter

7

Risk-Taking

Writers Develop by Stretching
Beyond What They Can Already Do

Sharing just six words can feel like a huge risk.

My eighth graders and I were huddled in the wings of the high school auditorium, stealing looks at the brightly lit stage we were about to step onto. Peeking out at the drum kits, the dozens of guitars resting in their stands, the microphones spaced out at the front edge of the stage. Our eyes were drawn to the taped marks on the floor where we would be standing when it was our time to sing, or solo, or read aloud our writing. We looked at each other wide-eyed, our minds replaying song lyrics, chord progressions, lines of poetry—all the things we had to remember when it was our turn. As we clustered backstage, our nervous energy and anticipation were as thick as the velvety curtains separating us from the audience—the audience we could hear filling the seats just beyond our hidden alcove.

There was plenty of risk-taking to go around.

We had just wrapped up the fall term, with my students crafting personal narratives and choice writing pieces in language arts and learning to play guitar for their first-quarter music class. For this culminating event, An Evening of Writing and Music, my eighth graders would be performing several songs, and everyone would be reading a piece of their writing. Some students had chosen longer pieces to share—memoirs, flash fiction, free-verse poems—but everyone would be reading at least six words.

We had been experimenting with six-word stories that fall—those pithy statements inspired by Hemingway's legendary microtale: "For sale: baby shoes, never worn." We had read countless examples from the Six-Word Memoirs project online and tried dozens of our own succinct statements about our lives, fears, hopes, and passions.

The six-word stories were grouped by theme and interspersed throughout the evening program, and every student shared one (See Figure 7–2). Some recounted their fondest memories:

The spray of powder, echoing skis.

Crack of the bat . . . ball soars!

Others captured everyday joys:

Rain boots, and dancing through storms.

Beautiful notes leaving my violin strings.

Some were inspirational mini-mantras that reflected challenges in their lives:

Asking for help doesn't mean weakness.

Failure is a work of art.

Learning it's okay to slow down.

Others were attempts to grapple with the wrongs in the world:

Why people with differences become outcasts?

Some expressed their deepest fears—past traumas or future worries:

Being so basic, I'm not heard.

Squeezing the surgeon's hand . . . lights out.

Some were poignant self-reflections:

I'm being crushed by the pressure.

You can't see past my walls.

For Kalen, who shared a longer narrative about the death of her grandfather, the risk she took was in first taking on the topic at all—in grappling with a subject that was personal and painful. She described the moment her mother received a phone call and told Kalen the news:

> The color of the room began to fade, the white walls started to turn into what looked like grey, angry clouds. The whole room was silent, the only thing I could hear was my heart pounding in my chest. I could feel her bed sheets start to crinkle in my hands as I grasped them in shock. My grandfather, my best friend for so many years, had passed.

For Alexa, there was huge risk in just stepping into the auditorium. Alexa was new to our school and still working on making social connections with classmates. She rarely made eye contact and was extremely self-conscious about her writing. She had tried some quickwriting in class but shook her head adamantly when any of us—peers or teachers—asked to take a peek. We invited her to join us for the evening program—even just to watch from the audience—but it seemed like a long shot.

I'm not sure how many people knew what it took for Alexa to join us there on the stage—the courage she had to summon—but when she uttered her six words, flanked by two supportive class-mates, the cheers sounded thunderous (see Figure 7–1).

Each of us had unique roles in the performance and different comfort levels with being on stage, but all of us were called upon to take risks—even yours truly. (I had been writing a short speech to kick off the program, which was now scribbled with last-minute revisions. There was also the matter of the '80s-rock guitar solo I was supposed to play during the finale—one I wasn't sure I could pull off.)

There was risk for all us in sharing our writing that night, but it was there

Figure 7–1 Alexa Takes a Risk

Figure 7–2   Taking Risks During Our
Evening of Writing and Music

throughout the writing process, as well. It's not easy to try a new genre or writing approach when we're not sure we'll be successful. We feel vulnerable when we're exploring a topic that's challenging—either because of the sensitive subject matter or because we aren't certain how we feel about it yet. Just putting the first words to a gaping blank page can feel like a risk.

But we want our writers to push at the boundaries of their perceived limits, don't we? As educators, we have certain skills to address, but our goal isn't  just to have students meet each standard—it's to have them grow along their own unique trajectories. We don't want the same writers at the end of the year that we had at the beginning. We want them to try something new—a different genre, point of view, text structure—even if they aren't sure how it will turn out. Writers with a risk-taking mindset are willing to live with uncertainty and a feeling of vulnerability; they question their written words and explore new revisions in search of something better. Rather than worry about getting it right, they stretch themselves with each new story, essay, or poem, from crafting it to sharing it.

But where does this willingness to risk come from—and what gets in its way? How can we foster this healthy risk-taking? (See Figure 7–3.)

Belief: Teachers Need to Acknowledge the Leaps of Faith

As teachers, we sometimes forget what a risk writing is for students—or anyone. It takes courage to reveal our writing to an audience—and even just to get our words on the page in the first place. And then *revising* them? With no guarantees and often no clear solutions, revision is a huge ask. Any stage of the process, from prewriting through publishing, can feel threatening in some way.

Risk is different for every student, every writer. For some, like Alexa, the notion of sharing our writing is terrifying, while others could belt out their first draft to a roomful of strangers with ease. The idea of trying a new genre or approach can be daunting for some; they know how to write a story, but a free-verse poem? *No way!* Fear of getting it wrong makes them hesitate to

Figure 7–3   Risk-Taking

veer off into fresh territory or diverge from the models they've seen. Risk is personal, and each of us has our own threshold.

So why take it on? Pushing past our limits helps us grow as writers. Taking a risk can be a thrill—a rush of excitement when we tackle a writing topic or project that intimidated us and it turns out better than we thought. Our readers laugh—or hold their breaths—at just the right moments. Instead of staying with the same old forms and moves, we branch out to something uncertain, and then we notice, with more than a touch of pride, that our writing looks different than it did before.

But that doesn't mean risk-taking is easy. To help students, we can acknowledge that writing risks exist but discuss how they help us grow. We can model risk-taking ourselves as teachers—and highlight other students who are stretching themselves. We can let students know that writing risks can be modest and should be on their own terms. We can create supportive structures and a safe environment in our classrooms.

Practice: Using Minilessons That Show a Range of Risks

After students have settled into your writing workshop—after they've gotten to know you and their peers and they've gotten comfortable with the routines and rhythms of your class—broach the subject of risk-taking. Ask them: "In what ways can writing be a risk?"

Have students respond with a quickwrite or turn-and-talk first, then transition to a class discussion about the different ways writing can be risky. You'll likely hear comments about how it takes a leap of faith to do any of the following:

- *Share our writing with others:* "It's a huge risk to share because what if no one liked my writing?" Momo said. "What if they all thought it was weird?" This fear of what others might say or how they might respond is often pervasive in my students' responses. "You want to express yourself but people might judge, and that can be embarrassing when you were trying your hardest," Ella said. According to Autumn, the threat of outside judgment looms large, no matter the writing. "Even if you're not spilling your guts out in a sad story, you're putting your humor, your words, your opinions out on display for people to see." Sharing writing in its early stages feels especially fraught. "It can be scary if you haven't shared it yet and this is your first time talking about this piece," Colin said. Some writers might allow a few confidantes to read their work, but the risk goes up exponentially when their audience expands to the full class—or beyond.

- *Take on a topic that is personal, painful, or challenging in some way:* Sometimes it's a subject that involves taking a position, one that everyone may not agree with. "You might be writing about something controversial, or you might be making a political statement," Cooper said, not long after our class had been writing responses to 2020 news events, such as Black Lives Matter protests and the contentious presidential election. Some writing might reveal parts of us we aren't certain we want laid bare. "When you're expressing your emotions and feelings, it can make you feel vulnerable and exposed," Mallory explained. The words we write might be ones we've never uttered aloud, even to ourselves. "It could be something you never talked about before," Grace said.

- *Try an unfamiliar writing task that's out of our comfort zone:* "It can be a risk to write in a different genre you don't normally write in," Rose said. Courtney agreed. "Experimenting with something new, or something you aren't used to with writing is hard." We might be asking students to try writing approaches or assignments that they aren't sure they can be successful with.

- *Revise our writing:* "It can be difficult sometimes—seeing what needs to be changed and getting ideas from other people," Courtney continued. It's a risk to alter our drafts when there's no set path—when we don't know if the revisions will make it any better. And cutting our writing—when it took so much to get the words down in the first place—can be agonizing. It's a risk to let go of parts we've written, even when we know our piece would be better off if we shed them. "A lot of times I write something good, but it just doesn't fit in the piece. It's still hard to cut it out and move on," Ginger said.

It helps to name and acknowledge these risks—and then invite students to take them anyway. Take your class' comments and categorize them (see Figure 7–4).

Practice: Using Minilessons That Model Risk-Taking

I know it's important to write alongside my students, and I often use my own drafts to model the writing process. I read a piece aloud and ask my students to give me feedback—for example, when I introduce conferring. Or I share a draft and describe some of my revisions as a way to model different craft moves.

Full confession though: sometimes my shares have been a bit of a sham.

I would dust off a writing piece from my archives—one I had already crafted and honed—and present it like it was still in process. I would show students the first draft and ask, "What are questions you are wondering about in my piece? Do you have some suggestions that could help me?" But I already knew the answers I wanted to hear. I had already worked through my revisions and had the polished draft waiting in the wings. Like a cooking-show host with

Risk Menu

Create a risk menu—a list of the ways we might try to stretch ourselves as writers:

▶ Try something unusual—an unfamiliar genre.

▶ Experiment with new writing moves (different types of endings, points of view, text structures, etc.).

▶ Write about a topic when you aren't sure how you feel about it yet or what your focus will be (when you're still figuring out your thoughts and feelings about it).

▶ Take on a writing piece you aren't certain you can pull off, for whatever reason.

▶ Write about a subject that challenges you (it might be personal, be painful, or take a stand).

▶ Cut out words, lines, and—*gasp*—whole sections you don't need.

▶ Start over! (Have a dud of a first draft? Take a risk to leave it behind and begin something fresh.)

▶ Share your piece with others. Consider getting feedback from different readers or sharing with a broader audience.

Figure 7–4   Risk Menu

a perfectly prepared dish just under the kitchen island, I would unveil my improvements a day or two later, as if to say, "Thanks to your feedback and the magic of ___ [insert writing strategy], look what I came up with! Voilà!"

I was asking students to take risks with their writing, but I was playing it safe. It was disingenuous, and it didn't model how tricky and uncertain revision can be. I needed to show my students my own willingness to stretch myself as writer.

Perhaps, like me, you could use a dose of authenticity in your own writing shares. To model the risk, try instead to follow the tips in Figure 7–5.

When we share writing in these ways, we're walking the walk—modeling the same risks we ask our students to embrace.

Share Without the Sham

▸ *Show students a draft of yours that's truly in process—imperfect and unpolished, warts and all.* **For example, I might say, "I asked you to try 'occasion poems'—a poem to mark a special event—so I thought I'd try one, too. I'm starting one about my daughter going away to college, but I'm struggling for a way to begin. It sounds a little sappy so far, like a greeting card."**

▸ *Present a piece of your writing that stretches you in some way. Share your genuine questions and wonderings with students.* **For example, "My go-to genre is personal narrative. Fiction scares me, though—I can invent interesting characters, but I always have a hard time thinking up a conflict for them. I'm worried the plot will fizzle out, so I usually avoid fiction writing. Even though I'm unsure how it'll turn out, I thought I would give it another try."**

▸ *Use a think-aloud to discuss some of the ways you are pushing your boundaries as you revise.* **For example, "Here's my draft essay about my birthmark. It's kind of a sensitive topic, since I'm describing how self-conscious I was of it as a kid—how it felt like a 'red stain' on my face, how it was 'a beacon blinking out my embarrassment.' Some of you asked how I feel about it now that I'm older and if I would have it removed, and it made me realize my feelings about my birthmark have changed and softened over time. I can't imagine life without it now. I hadn't really thought of how my attitude toward my birthmark has evolved, so I think I'll try to figure it out and include it in this piece somehow."**

Figure 7–5   Share Without the Sham

Practice: Using Mentor Texts That Feature Students Stretching Themselves

When we kick off a writing task, we often use mentor texts as models and inspiration. In addition to ones from published authors, we can include excerpts, examples, and anecdotes from students who have taken writing risks.

Your mentor texts will probably match whatever assignments you're asking students to try. For example, in writing personal narratives with my fifth graders, I have used a piece from my former student Tamiru, who wrote about being adopted from Ethiopia as a young child but knowing almost nothing about his background:

> When I was eight I asked my mom questions about my biological parents and she replied by telling me that she had files stashed away in her closet that had answers to my questions. She promised that she and I could look at them when I was older. Ever since, I've been building up questions about my past life, scratching and scratching the scar. It felt like it would never heal.

Tam built suspense as he zoomed in on one autumn night when he began to learn the answers:

> "Two years ago I made you a promise." I froze. Suddenly everything around me became silent. My head slowly turned to look at my mom. "Come on, I have something to show you."

Tam's piece is a worthy mentor text for many reasons—its use of metaphor, pacing, dialogue—but I also point out the risk he took in writing it. It wasn't easy grappling with feelings and questions that were deeply important to him—ones he tried to figure out through the writing. (See Figure 7–6.)

When sharing students' work, keep this in mind:

- Since students will see only the final product—the finished mentor text on the board or handout—be sure to describe the risks the writer took (which may be less obvious and unseen).

- It probably goes without saying, but we need to tread carefully with student work, especially when writers have taken a risk. Having students' permission to use their words as examples is paramount, as is being aware that some writing is best kept anonymous. Topics come up, especially with older writers, that need to be treated with caution (family difficulties, eating disorders, mental health challenges). Even with student consent, we want to think carefully about how and why—and if—we will share these with others.

Using Mentor Texts That Feature Students Taking Risks

Show your current students examples of how your previous ones have stretched themselves by

▸ trying unfamiliar or unusual writing tasks (whole new genres or approaches, blending or bending genres, etc.),

▸ cutting their writing,

▸ starting over or trying substantial revisions, or

▸ sharing their writing with a larger audience.

Figure 7–6   Using Mentor Texts That Feature Students Taking Risks

Practice: Sharing and Conferring to Support Risk-Taking

It's an emotional risk sharing something.
It might be something you've kept locked away for a while,
something that, up until now, was all yours.
—Katie, grade 8

If we want students to share their writing with us and their classmates, they have to know it's safe. Figure 7–7 includes some ideas and reminders for building the sense of community and connection that make risk-taking possible.

Sharing and Conferring That Supports Risk-Taking

▶ *Give students choice in* what *they share, and with* whom. **Let students decide whom to seek out for feedback. It might be a single partner or small group—or even someone outside of class. When you as a teacher do create conferring groups, be intentional and try to solicit student input. Ask: "Who would be a good fit for you as a conference partner? Who do you think would give you helpful feedback?" Allow students to choose** *what* **they share, as well. If they have a range of drafts—rather than a single required piece—they can select the writing (or section of writing) that feels ready for others' eyes.**

▶ *Teach students conferring structures that support risk-taking.* **Be explicit with students as you teach them how to confer and give feedback in ways that are nurturing and supportive.**

 ▪ *Give a predictable structure to follow,* **for example: (1) writer volunteers to read their piece aloud; (2) readers reflect and record comments; (3) readers respond out loud, beginning with strengths they notice, then giving questions and suggestions. When students know the format, they're more likely to feel it's safe to share.**

 ▪ *Teach how to give helpful feedback.* **As I discussed in Chapter 4, show students how to give comments that are specific and name the moves they see the writer making or at least attempting. Discuss and practice how to give questions and constructive advice as suggestions ("What if you tried . . . ?") rather than directives ("You should . . ."). Insist on comments that center on the writing (not the writer), are kind,** *and* **are genuine.**

▶ *Start slowly and monitor carefully before letting go.* **We want to give our students as much independence as possible, but they need scaffolding and practice before we set them loose to confer on their own.**
   Start with whole-group feedback; reinforce positive conferring behaviors you see; and make mental notes as you kidwatch. *How supportive are their comments to peers? How safe do students seem to feel?* **When they seem ready, give students more autonomy over their conferences (how they confer and with whom). It's not about holding on to teacher control; it's about establishing expectations for respect, kindness, specificity, and honesty.**

Figure 7–7 Sharing and Conferring That Supports Risk-Taking

Belief: Grades and Praise Can Undercut Risk-Taking

Grades can mess with our willingness to take a risk. Fear of getting a bad grade—or eagerness to get a good one—can lead us, as writers, to play it safe. We hew to our writing comfort zone—genres we know well, lines and themes we've heard our teacher or classmates use, drafts that mimic those we've seen modeled or that have worked for us in the past. We fixate on what the teacher wants—what she's looking for, what we need to get an A in his class—instead of trying something new.

As teachers, we sometimes dangle out grades as enticing carrots ("To get an A on this essay, you'll need at least five well-written paragraphs."), or we brandish them as sticks ("This piece is major part of your quarter grade, so be sure to stay on task this week!"). Whether we intend it or not, when grades are used as motivators, they can create anxiety—about either failure or having to repeat success—which can stifle risk-taking.

Some kinds of praise and feedback hamper risk-taking, as well. When we give vague kudos ("Great job!") or teacher-centered comments ("I love how you . . ."), we mean well, but it trains students to look to *us* for our judgments rather than learn how to evaluate effective writing for themselves. Rather than build their own sense of what's working—and where they might stretch themselves as writers—students turn to us for approval. As a teacher, I'm still working on moving away from giving out praise like this.

But don't writers need feedback? Don't they need to know what's working and what isn't? Absolutely. Our students need detailed feedback to grow—information about the strengths and places that need attention in their writing, especially as they're drafting. Rather than give general praise, though, it's important to identify the specific writing moves we see students making—what Peter Johnston calls "noticing and naming" (2004, 19). Instead of making comments that center on *our* judgments and what pleases *us*, we can be explicit about what we see our students trying, noting even the "partially correct" (Clay 1993). In fact, pointing out the effort we see our students making is key, according to Carol Dweck (2006). In her seminal research on mindset, Dweck discovered that when students were praised for their effort, they craved new, even difficult, tasks. Hard became *fun*. Students with this growth mindset "don't just *seek* challenge, they thrive on it," Dweck says. "The bigger the challenge, the more they stretch" (21).

Practice: Providing Assessment and Feedback That Support Risk-Taking

To help our students stretch as writers, we can emphasize certain types of assessment and feedback over others. (See Figure 7–8.)

Assessment and Feedback That Support Risk-Taking

Instead of . . .	Try to . . .
Giving a single overall score for a writing project (e.g., B+ or 88)	*Assess competencies without giving a final score.* Rather than assign an overall summative grade, consider assessments that give students more detailed feedback, such as rubrics and narratives. Assess writing in the different targeted areas described in your rubric (e.g., organization; evidence; word choice; narrative techniques)—perhaps with a rubric you developed together with your students. Use descriptors that give students a clearer sense of their progress in each identified area (e.g., meets or accomplished; in process or getting there; and beginning).
Focusing solely on content standards	*Give feedback related to the stances of a writer's mindset, including risk-taking.* Start by asking students to reflect on their risk-taking (or flexible thinking, transfer, etc.): "How did you take some risks and stretch yourself as a writer with this draft?" Try having your writers pause to consider their risk-taking *during* drafting, not just after the end. For example, "How might you take a risk and stretch yourself as you continue to revise? What might you try next (different organization, lead, ending, point of view)?"

Figure 7–8 Assessment and Feedback That Support Risk-Taking

(continues)

(continued)

Assessment and Feedback That Support Risk-Taking

Instead of . . .	Try to . . .
Grading the final product only	*Put emphasis on the writing process as well.* Create a writing process rubric (again, hopefully in collaboration with your students), acknowledging effort and the behaviors that make strong writing, and risk-taking, possible. Your process rubric might include items such as these: ▸ Reread and make changes while drafting. ▸ Seek out feedback from peers and teachers. ▸ Name, try out, and know the purpose of craft techniques. ▸ Listen to questions and suggestions from readers and try new approaches with a draft.
Focusing comments on external judgments ("I like the way you . . .") or general praise ("Good work!")	*Offer feedback grounded in specific observations:* ▸ Name the writing move or strategy you see students making. ("In your essay, I noticed you included lots of compelling facts about how oysters are so important to our bay.") ▸ Note the precise line or place in the writing where the student used it. ("You wrote how they filter up to forty gallons of water a day. That's a lot! You also used a powerful metaphor when you described oysters as 'the river's janitors.'") ▸ Share why this strategy or move improved the writing. ("The specific information you gave will really convince readers we need oysters, and show them why we should build more oyster reefs in Great Bay.")

Shifts in assessment and feedback, like the ones in Figure 7–8, bolster our willingness to risk—for our students and for all of us as writers.

My friend Mike Anderson recently taught a university course for language arts educators and wanted these adults—some of whom expressed anxiety about taking a graduate-level class—to write a personal narrative. "You all have an A already," he assured them, and then they discussed the primary goal: to try something out of their comfort zones—to take the kind of writing risks we encourage our students to take. As they drafted over the next few days, the teachers experimented with their writing, gauging for themselves what approaches were working and what needed changing in their emerging pieces. "No one was asking, 'Is this what you're looking for?'" Mike said.

At the final share, one teacher wrote his self-portrait in the form of a recipe. Another, a first-grade teacher, composed a *Hamilton*-style rap about growing up with a learning disability. "There's no way they would have tried those things if they had been worried about grades," Mike said. "Taking a risk was the goal, and they nailed it!" Without the fear of doing poorly in his course, all of Mike's students ventured out on different limbs, crafting pieces that were inventive, powerful, and moving.

While Mike's exact approach may not be one you take in your classroom, we can take inspiration from it. We can de-emphasize grades and teacher-centered comments—and center risk-taking as the goal.

Belief: Confusing Revision with Editing Dampens Risk-Taking

When Molly first arrived in my class and I asked her what she knew about revision, she described it as "editing and fixing pieces of writing to make them . . . efficient and official." Maggie said, "Revision is what you do to fix your mistakes; spelling, grammar, punctuation, etc." For Dominic, revision was "just looking over the work to make sure there aren't any errors." (See Figures 7–9 and 7–10.)

Figure 7–9   Molly's Survey

What is revision? What does revision mean to you?

Revision is editing and fixing peices of writing to make them offcial. Revision is making writing afficiant and official.

Figure 7–10   Maggie's Survey

What is revision? What does revision mean to you?

Rivision is what you do to fix your mistakes; Spelling, grammer, punchuation, ect.

When students—or teachers—conflate editing and revision, it has real consequences. Using *revise* and *edit* interchangeably may seem like a trifling matter, but it has big implications on how we view writing. When we mix these two up, we think of revision as "fixing mistakes" or hunting for errors. We think it's about searching for things that are *wrong* in our writing.

When students think of revision as avoiding errors, it puts them in a deficit mindset, trying to prevent problems rather than playing with possibilities. This kind of thinking focuses on faults, which would squelch anyone's impulse to try something new. But there's no formula for strong writing, no algorithm for revision. We can't think and write outside the box if we perceive good writing as something that never strays from the confines of the box itself.

If we want our students to take risks with their writing and revisions, we can't have them hung up on finding *the* right way. We have to remind them that revision involves discovering *a* fresh path—not *the* way forward—and that there are lots of potential approaches to experiment and play with a draft.

Since revision and editing have a nagging habit of getting lumped together, we need to help students keep them separate. "Construct a brick wall between the two!" Ralph Fletcher and JoAnn Portalupi say (2001, 66). Of course, editing is important in its own right, and we should give it its due, but we shouldn't allow it to be confused with its—*ahem*, more important—cousin, revision.

Practice: Using Minilessons That Build a Wall Between Revision and Editing

Discuss the difference between revision and editing with your students. See Figure 7–11 for some ideas to try as you build a wall between them.

After this minilesson and throughout your year, be careful with your language to keep revision and editing distinct. Teach separate minilessons for both revision and editing skills and be clear to distinguish between the two (and gently remind students to do the same). Doing so doesn't guarantee students will take writing risks, but it sends a message: revision isn't probing a piece for errors or following a set of rules but exploring the possibilities and our range of choices as writers.

Ways to Teach the Differences Between Revision and Editing

During a minilesson, ask, "What's the difference between revision and editing?" Draw out students' initial ideas about these practices (including their misperceptions), and then build two distinct lists together.

▶ *Discuss the different purposes and processes of editing and revision.* Some ideas that may emerge:

- We edit to make sure our ideas are clear and understandable for others (and even us). Editing involves checking our spelling, mechanics, and punctuation (such as periods to end sentences and quotation marks to show talking), so our writing is easy to read, in just the way we intended.
- We revise to find the focus of our writing, express our ideas more clearly, develop our thoughts more fully, and discover what we truly want to say. Revision involves adding, reorganizing, changing words and whole sections, and deleting parts we don't need.

▶ *Use metaphors, similes, or other ways to explain and show students the difference.* You might say, "Editing is like the road signs and traffic lights of your writing. They signal to readers where to stop, where new ideas are merging, where drivers need to tap the breaks. Revision is like constructing whole new towns and landscapes. It's like building a city in the sand at the beach, with us deciding where to put the buildings, tunnels, and roads—knocking some down and building new ones where we want them."

Or you could say, "Editing is fixing problems with your car during its inspection (tires, lights, exhaust system); revision is designing the vehicle itself (creating a Porsche or a pickup)."

▶ *Use quotes or videos from favorite authors that illustrate ideas about revision or editing.* For example, I might share this quote from Eve Bunting to show her revision process:

> I always read my work aloud, making myself aware of how it sounds. Do the words flow pleasantly? Do they evoke vibrant images? I check for over-writing. Does the dialogue sound real?

Figure 7–11 Ways to Teach the Differences Between Revision and Editing   *(continues)*

(continued)

I have written, "I know I am well loved." I, the author, might say that. But would my protagonist, the one who is speaking in my book? He's a fourteen-year-old boy. Come on, Eve. Get real! (McClure and Kristo 1996, 224–25)

Discussing this quote with students gives us an opportunity to talk about how revision involves reading our draft aloud, listening for how it sounds and the images it (hopefully) conjures, and striving for the right voice. Find other quotes about revision and writing and use them in your writing workshop from time to time to highlight different aspects of revision or editing.

▶ *Emphasize the agency and choices students have with revision.* Revision checklists are fine, of course, but if we want students to write authentically, we shouldn't prescribe their assignments too restrictively (e.g., every paragraph needs three supporting details; your poem needs five "juicy adjectives").

Note: Many grammar gurus out there will argue that editing—not just revision—can involve creativity, decision-making, and even play. They would tell us that writers can make choices, not just follow rules, with the mechanics of a draft. They would rightly point out that writers sometimes bend the rules of grammar for effect (e.g., using a well-placed sentence fragment; employing a one-sentence—or even one-word—paragraph; using incorrect grammar to show voice). True. Even still, editing does involve learning—and generally adhering to—certain guidelines.

Belief: Teachers Need to Highlight the Rewards of Risk and Make It Inviting

Just its name, *risk*, sounds like something we'd want to avoid, reduce, or prevent. When we look it up, *risk* means "the possibility of loss or injury; danger; peril" (Merriam-Webster). By taking a risk, we cause ourselves stress—another word with negative connotations. *We want to shed all stress and risk in our lives, don't we?*

Not so, experts say. Stress can be toxic when it becomes overwhelming—when it's chronic, traumatic, or the load is too large for us to handle. We're in "dis-stress." But there is also something researchers call "eustress"—the discomfort we feel when we have a big test or writing project (Jain 2015). These "good stresses," psychologists say, are just part of a normal, healthy life; clearing away all stress and risk for our students isn't possible or desirable. "'Avoiding stress doesn't work,'" says Jeremy P. Jamieson, an associate professor of psychology. "'We have to get outside our comfort zones and approach challenges'" (Damour 2018).

We inherently know this—that to grow we can't stay stagnant or stick to the same things we've always tried. We recognize it takes lifting weights or running an extra lap to build our muscles or stamina. The challenge can't be too big—we shouldn't take on a marathon when we've just taken up jogging—but tasks that are too easy don't help either. Vygotsky's zone of proximal development—the notion that we need to aim for just-right risks, the ones right at our developmental level—makes sense to us.

One key step, researchers say, is changing how students themselves regard these everyday stresses. Our perception of stress matters (Damour 2018). If students can learn to see some stress and risk as a healthy, albeit uncomfortable, sign of growth, it can have "powerful downstream effects," psychologist Lisa Damour (2018) says. Students are more likely to take future risks and do better on challenging tasks compared with students who see all risk and stress as negative. According to Damour, "Studies of teenagers found that when faced with steep intellectual tasks, individuals with a stress-is-enhancing outlook outperform those with a stress-is-debilitating one" (2018).

Students get this—though, like all of us, they sometimes need reminders. The morning after our writing and guitar performance, I asked my classes about the stress they felt and whether the risk was worth it. "Writing is nerve-wracking for me," Will said, "but some stress is helpful. It means you care about the writing and you want it to be as good as you can. Some stress can make you do better, and then you feel better after the fact." Hailea agreed, noting that reading our work in front of an audience gave us a jolt of "adrenaline" and "overall it upped our performance." Kalen, who wrote the piece about her grandfather's death, said reading it to an audience was "scary but exciting." Taking the risk to write and share such a personally significant piece "helps you do your best," she said.

As teachers, it helps to highlight how some risks—at the right level, on our own terms—can be helpful, and we can invite students to take them on when they're ready.

Practice: Using Minilessons That Show Risk as Growth

In a minilesson, introduce the idea of comfort, growth, and panic zones to students. (See Figure 7–12.)

Represent these zones visually with a set of concentric circles, perhaps marking them on your classroom floor. (See Figure 7–13.) After explaining the zones, give students a series of scenarios and ask: "Where would you be in this situation—in your comfort, growth, or panic zone?" After each question, have students vote with their feet by moving into the circle on the floor that fits them for each scenario.

Start with nonacademic examples. Ask students how much of a risk would it be for them to:

- ride a rollercoaster

- sing a solo on stage

- move to a new school

- have the last at-bat or penalty kick in a tied baseball or soccer game.

Comfort, Growth, and Panic Zones

▶ The comfort zone is our emotional state when we're experiencing activities we know well. It's stress-free and secure, but it can be stagnant and boring.

▶ The growth zone is where we're at when we're trying new experiences, some that excite and challenge us. It involves some risk and stress but at a level that can be exhilarating (though a bit uncomfortable at first). We learn and grow in this zone, often taking our performance to the next level.

▶ The panic zone is where stress gets overwhelming. We step into this zone when we're thrust into a risk that's too big. We feel fear and anxiety, and our performance decreases.

Figure 7–12   Comfort, Growth, and Panic Zones

Next, move on to writing-related examples. How much of a risk would it be for them to do one of the following?

- read aloud their writing in front of a small group

- read aloud their writing in front of a larger audience

- get suggestions on their writing from someone who's not a close friend

- cut parts out of a story they've written

- start a piece over from scratch

- write in a new genre they've never tried before

- write about something when they aren't sure how they feel about it yet

Pause during or after the activity to discuss the risk level students felt for different tasks. As part of your debriefing, touch on the following points:

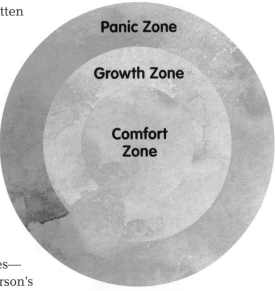

Figure 7–13 The Zones Represented Visually

- The same activity can prompt different reactions—different zones—depending on the person. One person's comfort-zone activity hits another person's panic button. Risk is individual.

- We can expand our growth zone. When we try new things and gain new experiences, our growth zone stretches. What used to seem scary or impossible becomes fun and doable.

- When we take on a risk in our growth zone, it often has powerful benefits and rewards. For some of the writing risks your students might take, ask: "What rewards might you get from taking a risk like this? Why might it be worth it?"

- For example, you might say, "I noticed sharing our writing is a definite risk for many of us. Lots of you stepped into the growth or panic zones on that one! Why do you think it might be a risk that's worth taking sometimes though?" Students might offer ideas such as these:

- "We get to see how our writing affects other people. It feels good to see them laugh at the funny lines or get excited at suspenseful ones I put in."

- "When readers are confused or have questions, it helps us to know what parts might still be unclear."

- "It's a little scary, but knowing someone else might read it makes us work on it to make it better."

- "Other readers might give me ideas I hadn't thought about before—things I could add and even ones I did well and didn't realize."

This activity gives you a visual representation of your students' risk-taking with writing. It can also be a powerful discussion starter for why some stress and risk can help us grow.

Practice: Drafting and Revising by Inviting Students to Take a Risk

Pose this question occasionally to your students: "What's a risk you might take with this piece of writing?" Revisit the risk menu you and your class brainstormed and have students consider some ways they might push themselves, even in a small way. Your invitation to risk could be informal and brief or part of a longer writing reflection. The timing can be just as students are starting a draft or when they're in the middle of revising it. Your invitation to risk could take different forms:

- a group discussion

- a turn-and-talk

- an exit slip

- a longer written reflection

Whatever form you choose, extending an invitation to risk will lead many writers to stretch their boundaries a bit. When I asked my eighth graders to write a piece that shared something about them, I invited them to take a risk in any area: genre, topic, revision strategies, whom they'd share with, and so on. The breadth and depth of their writing—and the risks they took—were inspiring. A few examples:

- Gabby chose to face a painful memory—her father's heart attack two years earlier—capturing some of the ways this traumatic event shaped her and her family. In several powerful passages, she described her shock at first hearing the news:

> I can't feel, I can't move. I feel like I'm falling down a well and I don't know what to do. . . . I hear a slight murmur of my mom still talking but I can't listen. I have so many questions. *What caused it? Why today? . . . What if he doesn't come home?*

- Elsa tried an unusual form of narrative writing: an obituary. It wasn't a genre our class had ever tried, and yet Elsa, a conscientious student who generally stuck close to expected guidelines, chose to step out of her comfort zone. In her piece, she reflected on her passions, goals, and favorite memories, but through this different form:

> Two weeks of her summers were spent on Lake Ossipee at Camp Nellie Huckins. Elsa attended camp for five summers, where she loved swimming, singing on tables, and convincing her friends to sneak out to look at the stars.

- Rose started a short story about a little girl saving her cherished blanket—much like her own treasured blanket as a child—from a fire, but she felt it just wasn't coming together during revision. Middraft, she took the risk to cut her losses and start anew, taking a different approach to a similar topic. Rose saved one section and transformed it into a series of poetic vignettes, showing a blanket's journey, starting with a baby girl's first memories:

> Waa waaaaa
> Soft fabric against my face

Arms hugging me tight

Bright room

Full of noise, the world

In the stanzas that follow, the blanket moves through the girl's life, as she takes it surreptitiously to school and then, later as an adult, passes it along to her own daughter:

The bow is in place, pink wrapping paper folded neatly

I hug the box to my chest

Remembering my life with it

The scent of the blanket lingers . . .

It is ready to go, onto a new life.

• Easton chose the most personal of topics—coming out to their family as agender. Easton wrote in the mode of fan fiction modeled after the Japanese manga characters they love (complete with superpowers and complex backstories). As part of the piece, Yaku, the main character who was born female, comes out to their parents as agender, hoping for acceptance. Yaku nervously rehearses ways to bring up the subject:

I wonder if I could ask for more boyish clothes—what would Mom think? Should I say it straight up or just beat around the bush? "*Hey Mom, I have something to tell you . . .* "? No, that's too straightforward. "*So, I have something I would like to inform you about . . .* "? God, no! It sounds like I'm a doctor giving bad news. . . .

Some elements were true to Easton's life, and others were inspired by fiction, but it took a risk to commit them to the page (not to mention to meld genres in such an unusual way).

When inviting students to risk, keep the following in mind:

- *Put students in the driver's seat; let them decide what kind of risk is right for them.* It helps to know our students well—who seems ready for a nudge and who needs more reassurance—but they know themselves best. Let them choose the risks they take as writers.

- *Adjust your expectations for risk-taking.* Even risks that are seemingly small to us as teachers can feel huge for students. I cringe thinking about the times I tossed students together for impromptu conferences before they were ready (and then wondered why their conversations were so strained). Or when I suggested lengthy lists of revisions and was baffled when students attempted only a few. Even modest revisions and risks can be monumental; they're cumulative and gather momentum over time. Revisions *should* be substantive—not just window dressing—but they don't have to be extreme makeovers either.

- *Don't rush risk-taking.* It takes time and care to develop the trust that's required—this doesn't happen on week one! Allow time for students to get to know one another and you. As they gradually learn your class' routines and structures—and recognize they are well supported and safe—they'll venture out. (See Figure 7–14.)

Figure 7–14 Invite Students to Choose Their Own Risks

A Final Invitation

I once had the good fortune to have Don Murray visit my class. Don lived down the street from me in Durham, New Hampshire, and he graciously agreed to be interviewed by my fifth graders and join us for our workshop time. Though most known as a Pulitzer Prize–winning journalist and renowned columnist, Don was in the thick of exploring poetry and drawing in his retirement, and he brought several pieces to share. As he presented one poem about his experiences as a paratrooper in France during World War II, one of my students asked if he would revise it. "Oh yes," he said. "I'll probably revise it sixty or seventy times before I'm satisfied."

To me, this comment—casually mentioned by someone who championed and lived the writing process—was inspirational. Judging by the stunned expressions on some students' faces, though, not everyone felt invigorated and fired up by the thought of dozens and dozens of drafts ahead.

For our students—for all writers—even a little revision can feel like a lot.

As writing teachers, we want our students to embrace revision with zeal, but perhaps it's enough that they appreciate it—that they feel, in the words of my student Molly, that "revision means hard work, but it's worth it." There are times we want our young writers to overhaul their drafts, but maybe it's enough that they make a few modest but consequential changes.

Revision doesn't have to be radical.

The same is true for you as an educator reading this book. All the stances and practices you've just read aren't intended as a recipe to follow or an outline to revamp your entire language arts program. Instead, it's a smorgasbord to sample from and an invitation to shake a few things up. As I said, no writer—fourth grader or Faulkner—embodies all the stances, all the time, and it isn't possible—certainly not advisable—to teach all the activities included here in a single year, with the same group of students.

So, I invite you to begin where I did years ago with my teacher research—with a question or two. This book emerged out of an action-research project, stemming from a couple of genuine questions: "What's behind revision resistance—'I like it the way it is'? How can I help my student writers move past it?" My language arts classes became a learning laboratory, where we tried—and continue to try—different approaches to create a culture of revision. The questions have helped us find ways to make revision more authentic, engaging, meaningful, and fun.

Observe your writers and the strengths and needs you see. Consider designing your own research question related to one of the stances in a writer's mindset. Perhaps it's optimism: *How can I get my students to see what's working with their writing (especially those who struggle to stay positive)?* Maybe you'll focus on flexible thinking: *What strategies would help my writers stay open to changes as they're drafting and revising (instead of rushing to "The End")?* You might start with tensions you notice during your writing workshop, the students who keep you up at night, or perhaps a classroom observation that surprises you.

As you dive into your own inquiries about your students' writing mindsets, you'll be adopting the same stances you're teaching. It will require you to *take risks* and *think flexibly*—to try different approaches and reexamine parts of your standard teaching repertoire. You'll have to *transfer* your knowledge of kids and best practices to new situations. You will certainly step into your students' shoes and *take their perspective* as you figure out what's helping them improve as writers. You'll have to be *optimistic*—to focus and build on the strategies that work well (and let the inevitable blunders go). As you reflect on what you've tried—the specific activities included in these chapters or the ones you're inspired to dream up on your own—you'll be thinking *metacognitively*.

You will be living the stances as you teach them. You'll be revising *yourself* as you teach your students about revision. I hope you'll accept the invitation.

References

Alexander, Kwame. 2016. *Booked*. New York: HarperCollins.

Anderson, Carl. 2018. *A Teacher's Guide to Writing Conferences*. Portsmouth, NH: Heinemann.

Atwell, Nancie. 1998. *In the Middle: New Understandings About Writing, Reading, and Learning*. Portsmouth, NH: Boynton/Cook.

Ballenger, Bruce. 1990. "The Importance of Writing Badly." *The Christian Science Monitor*, March 28, 18.

Baty, Chris. 2004. *No Plot? No Problem! A Low-Stress, High-Velocity Guide to Writing a Novel in 30 Days*. San Francisco: Chronicle Books.

Bomer, Katherine. 2010. *Hidden Gems: Naming and Teaching from the Brilliance in Every Student's Writing*. Portsmouth, NH: Heinemann.

Calkins, Lucy McCormick. 1986. *The Art of Teaching Writing*. Portsmouth, NH: Heinemann.

Clay, Marie. 1993. *Reading Recovery: A Guidebook for Teachers in Training*. Portsmouth, NH: Heinemann.

Collins, Billy. 1988. "Introduction to Poetry." In *The Apple That Astonished Paris*, 58. Fayetteville: University of Arkansas Press.

Costa, Arthur L., and Bena Kallick, eds. 2008. *Learning and Leading with Habits of Mind: 16 Essential Characteristics for Success*. Alexandria, VA: ASCD.

Damour, Lisa. 2018. "How to Help Teenagers Embrace Stress." *The New York Times*, September 19. https://www.nytimes.com/2018/09/19/well/family/how-to-help-teenagers-embrace-stress.html.

Dweck, Carol S. 2006. *Mindset: The New Psychology of Success*. New York: Ballantine Books.

Elbow, Peter. 1973. *Writing Without Teachers*. New York: Oxford University Press.

———. 2012. *Vernacular Eloquence: What Speech Can Bring to Writing*. New York: Oxford University Press.

Elbow, Peter, and Pat Belanoff. 1995. *Sharing and Responding*. New York: McGraw Hill.

Fletcher, Ralph. 2017. *Joy Write: Cultivating High-Impact, Low-Stakes Writing*. Portsmouth, NH: Heinemann.

Fletcher, Ralph, and JoAnn Portalupi. 2001. *Writing Workshop: The Essential Guide*. Portsmouth, NH: Heinemann.

Gallagher, Kelly, and Penny Kittle. 2018. *180 Days: Two Teachers and the Quest to Engage and Empower Adolescents*. Portsmouth, NH: Heinemann.

Glover, Matt. 2020. *Craft and Process Studies: Units That Provide Writers with Choice of Genre*. Portsmouth, NH: Heinemann.

Heard, Georgia. 2002. *The Revision Toolbox: Teaching Techniques That Work.* Portsmouth, NH: Heinemann.

Jain, Renee. 2015. "Can Stress Help Students?" Edutopia. George Lucas Educational Foundation. February 9. https://www.edutopia.org/blog /can-stress-help-students-renee-jain.

Janeczko, Paul B, comp. 2002. *Seeing the Blue Between: Advice and Inspiration for Young Poets.* Cambridge, MA: Candlewick Press.

Johnston, Peter H. 2004. *Choice Words: How Our Language Affects Children's Learning.* Portland, ME: Stenhouse.

Kuhl, Patricia. 2010. "The Linguistic Genius of Babies." Filmed in October at TEDxRainier, Seattle, Washington. TED video, 10:01. https://www.ted.com /talks/patricia_kuhl_the_linguistic_genius_of_babies.

Lane, Barry. 2016. *After The End: Teaching and Learning Creative Revision.* Portsmouth, NH: Heinemann.

Lafferty, Mur. 2017. "NaNo Prep: Make a Box for Your Bully." *The NaNoWriMo Blog*, September 20. https://blog.nanowrimo.org/post/165551897886 /a-box-for-your-bully-mur-lafferty-im-writing-a.

Mraz, Kristine, and Christine Hertz. 2015. *A Mindset for Learning: Teaching the Traits of Joyful, Independent Growth.* Portsmouth, NH: Heinemann.

McClure, Amy A., and Janice V. Kristo, eds. 1996. *Books That Invite Talk, Wonder, and Play.* Urbana, IL: NCTE.

Merriam-Webster Dictionary, s.v. "risk." Accessed June 24, 2021, https://www .merriam-webster.com/dictionary/risk.

Murray, Donald M. 1990. *Shoptalk: Learning to Write with Writers.* Portsmouth, NH: Boynton/Cook.

———. 2001. *The Craft of Revision.* Fort Worth, TX: Harcourt College Publishers.

Park, Barbara. 1995. *Mick Harte Was Here.* New York: Scholastic.

Rief, Linda. 2014. *Read Write Teach: Choice and Challenge in the Reading-Writing Workshop.* Portsmouth, NH: Heinemann.

Romano, Tom. 2000. *Blending Genre, Altering Style: Writing Multigenre Papers.* Portsmouth, NH: Heinemann.

Sehgal, Parul. 2021. "George Saunders Conducts a Cheery Class on Fiction's Possibilities." *The New York Times*, updated January 19. https://www .nytimes.com/2021/01/12/books/review-swim-pond-rain-george-saunders .html.

Shagoury, Ruth, and Brenda Miller Power. 2012. *Living the Questions: A Guide for Teacher Researchers.* Portland, ME: Stenhouse Publishers.

Willems, LaDonna, and Chris Baty. 2020. "101,572 words in 30 days." Dropbox Design. Dropbox. February 4. https://dropbox.design/article/101-572 -words-in-30-days.

Worth, Valerie. 1987. *All the Small Poems.* New York: Farrar, Straus, and Giroux.